Rethinking Children's Rights

Attitudes in Contemporary Society

Phil Jones and Susan Welch

New Childhoods Series

continuum

Continuum International Publishing Group

The Tower Building   80 Maiden Lane
11 York Road   Suite 704
London SE1 7NX   New York, NY 10038

www.continuumbooks.com

British Library Cataloguing-in-Publication Data
A catalogue record for this book is available from the British Library.

ISBN: 9781441195401 (hardcover)
      9781847063243 (paperback)

Library of Congress Cataloging-in-Publication Data
Jones, Phil.
Rethinking children's rights / Phil Jones and Susan Welch.
p. cm.
ISBN: 978-1-4411-9540-1
ISBN: 978-1-84706-324-3
1. Children's rights. I. Welch, Susan. II. Title.
HQ789.J66 2009
323.3'52–dc22

                            2009035015

Typeset by Newgen Imaging Systems Pvt Ltd, Chennai, India
Printed and bound in Great Britain by the MPG Books Group

Rethinking Children's Rights

WITHDRAWN

Companion Website available

The Companion Website relating to this book is available online at:
http://education.welch.continuumbooks.com

Please visit the link and register with us to receive your password and access to the Companion Website.

If you experience any problems accessing the Companion Website, please contact Continuum at info@continuumbooks.com.

Other books in the *New Childhoods* series

Rethinking Childhood, Phil Jones
Rethinking Children and Families, Nick Frost
Rethinking Children and Research, Mary Kellett
Rethinking Children, Violence and Safeguarding, Lorraine Radford
Rethinking Children's Play, Fraser Brown and Michael Patte
Rethinking Gender and Sexuality in Childhood, Emily W. Kane

Also available from Continuum

Respecting Childhood, Tim Loreman
Whose Childhood Is It, Richard Eke, Helen Butcher and Mandy Lee
Education and Construction of Childhood, David Blundell

Contents

Introduction to New Childhoods Series   ix

Part 1 DEBATES, DILEMMAS AND CHALLENGES: THE BACKGROUND TO CHILDREN'S RIGHTS

1 Introduction to *Rethinking Children's Rights*   3

Introduction and key questions   3

Do societies see child rights in different ways?   4

What do the different responses to the UNCRC reveal?   6

What issues are emerging in relation to rethinking children's rights?   13

How can negative responses to the rights agenda be used to help rethink children's rights?   21

Summary   27

2 Children's Rights: definitions and developments   29

Introduction and key questions   29

Is there a common understanding of the term 'right'?   30

What differences exist in relation to children's rights?   34

How can the history of children's rights help us understand current issues?   40

How do ideas about adult–child relationships affect thinking about children's rights?   48

What does research tell us about the state of children's rights internationally and in the United Kingdom?   51

Summary   55

Further reading   56

Research details   56

Part 2 AN INTERDISCIPLINARY REVIEW OF RECENT RESEARCH AND SCHOLARSHIP

3 Children's Rights: current tensions, debates and research   61
Introduction and key questions   61
What are current, emerging tensions and debates in relation to children's rights?   62
What are some of the implications of these tensions?   66
What is research showing us about tensions and debates concerning children's rights?   73
Summary   80
Further reading   81
Research details   81

Part 3 IMPLICATIONS FOR CHILDREN'S LIVES

4 Rights and the 'Child's Voice'   85
Introduction and key questions   85
What is the meaning of 'child's voice'?   86
How does 'voice' relate to rights?   90
What is research revealing about rights-informed practices relating to voice and participation?   95
Summary   108
Further reading   108
Research details   108

5 Rights and Decision Making   110
Introduction and key questions   110
In what ways does decision making feature in children's lives?   111
What is the relationship between children's rights and decision making?   114
What tensions are emerging concerning decision making and children?   116
What does research reveal about the impact of new thinking and practice in relation to rights and decision making in different spaces within children's lives?   125
Summary   132
Further reading   132
Research details   133

6 **A Rights Perspective on Family Life** 135

Introduction and key questions 135

Is there a relationship between children, their families and rights? 136

Can the family support children's rights? 137

How do economic, social and political factors affect families
in relation to rights? 139

What is the role of the state in relation to carers, children and
their rights? 152

How can we understand the relationship between children,
families and rights? 157

Summary 159

Further reading 160

Research details 160

7 **Working with Children** 163

Introduction and key questions 163

In what kind of contexts does work with children occur? 164

What rights issues arise for those working with children? 167

What can research tell us about what children want from those
who work with them? 172

What positive examples are there of working with children? 175

Summary 182

Further reading 182

Research details 182

References 184
Index 191

Introduction to New Childhoods Series

The amount of current attention given to children and to childhood is *rapid pace of change* unprecedented. Recent years have seen the agreement of new international conventions, national bodies established and waves of regional and local initiatives all concerning children.

This rapid pace has been set by many things: from children themselves, from adults working with children, from governments and global bodies, injustice, and dissatisfaction, new ideas and raw needs are fuelling change. Within and, often, leading the movement is research. From the work of multi-national corporations designed to reach into the minds of children and the pockets of parents, through to charity-driven initiatives aiming to challenge the forces that situate children in extreme poverty, a massive amount of energy is expended in research relating to children and their lives. This attention is not all benign. Research can be seen as original investigation undertaken in order to gain knowledge and understanding through a systematic and rigorous process of critical enquiry examining 'even the most commonplace assumption' (Kellett, 2005, 9). However, as Kellett has pointed out, the findings can be used by the media to saturate and accost, rather than support, under 12s who are obese, for example, or to stigmatize young people by the use of statistics. However, research can also play a role in investigating, enquiring, communicating and understanding. Recent years have seen innovations in the focus of research, as political moves that challenge the ways in which children have been silenced and excluded result in previously unseen pictures of children's experiences of poverty, family life, community. The attitudes, opinions and lived experiences of children are being given air, and one of the themes within this book concerns the opportunities and challenges this is creating. As this book will reveal, research is being used to set new agendas, to challenge ways of living and working that oppress, harm or limit children. It is also being used to test preconceptions and long-held beliefs about children's lived experiences, the actual effects rather than the adult's opinions of the way parents see and relate to their children or the actual impact of services and their ways of working with children.

In addition to the focus of research, innovations are being made in the way research is conceived and carried out. Its role in children's lives is changing. In the past much research treated children as objects; research was done on them, with the agenda and framework set purely by adults. New work is emerging where children create the way research is conceived and carried out. Children act as researchers and researchers work with questions formulated by children or work with children.

This series aims to offer access to some of the challenges, discoveries and work-in-progress of contemporary research. The terms 'child' and 'childhood' are used within the series in line with Article 1 of the United Nations Convention on the Rights of the Child which defines 'children' as persons up to the age of 18. The books offer opportunities to engage with emerging ideas, questions and practices. They will help those studying childhood or those living and working with children to become familiar with challenging work, in order to engage with their findings and reflect on their own ideas, experiences and ways of working.

Phil Jones
Leeds University

Part 1
Debates, Dilemmas and Challenges: the background to children's rights

Introduction to *Rethinking Children's Rights*

Chapter Outline

Introduction and key questions   3

Do societies see child rights in different ways?   4

What do the different responses to the UNCRC reveal?   6

What issues are emerging in relation to rethinking children's rights?   13

How can negative responses to the rights agenda be used to help rethink children's rights?   21

Summary   27

Introduction and key questions

The idea and the practice of rights for children has emerged over recent years as a powerful force in children's lives. In many societies it is a catalyst for positive changes within the ways adults and children live and work together. The pictures emerging from research reveal that the impetus, or dynamic, created by child rights is being engaged with in order to transform lives in positive directions. In addition, research also reveals that frictions, problems and failures are occurring in creating such changes and that these are harmful to children and their communities.

The cornerstone for most contemporary definitions, developments, or discussion is the United Nations Convention on the Rights of the Child (UNCRC, 1989). As Chapters 2 and 3 will discuss in more detail, this has tended to be divided into different areas of rights. One framework approaches rights in terms of liberty rights and welfare rights; another often-used analysis sees them as concerned with discourses of provision, protection and participation. After over two decades of responses to the UNCRC it is possible to *rethink* child rights in the light of contemporary research into what has occurred so far? This book attempts to answer this question by examining key aspects of the journey made to date and by looking forward to the future possibilities of the impetus that is being created by children's rights.

> Do societies see child rights in different ways?
> What do the different responses to the UNCRC reveal?
> What issues are emerging in relation to rethinking children's rights?
> How can negative responses to the rights agenda be used to help rethink children's rights?

Do societies see child rights in different ways?

A convention developed by a body such as the United Nations involves certain kinds of perspectives on rights. These are international in scope, and the UNCRC has been ratified by most individual nations. Ratification means that an individual government undertakes to implement the UNCRC recommendations in its laws and policies and to report to the United Nations Committee on the Rights of the Child on the progress being made. The Committee issues reports, and other non-government organizations also use the UNCRC as a framework for making their own reports on a country's response to child rights and on the lives of children. Chapter 2 will review how definitions, ideas and practices concerning child rights have emerged and will show how they are reflected in relation to the specific details of the UNCRC. The purpose of this book is to foreground experiences in the United Kingdom with references to responses in a variety of countries as an approach to understanding the nature of the *emerging relationships* between child rights as a *concept* and their *implementation* in practice.

One of the emerging themes involves the *kinds* of responses that have occurred within different countries as the international convention comes into contact with the enthusiasms and frustrations created by national governments or localized practices and attitudes. The UNCRC may make a series of statements in its Articles, but these are only as good as the way an individual country or society responds to them.

Different phenomena come into play within these responses: the idea of child rights, for example, does not exist in a pure vacuum of ideal and child-centred philosophy. Within individual countries, and in cultures and communities that make up those countries, research is revealing different issues that are foregrounded in children's lives and the ways in which ideas of child rights have developed their own localised meanings and drivers for change. These driving forces, ideas and interpretations are created by interactions between the nature of the society and communities children live within and the wishes or intentions of children, young people and adults, acting individually and in groups. Viewed in this way, it becomes useful to see what these can tell us about the ways the notion of child rights is changing and developing: what people want and intend – the variations of difference created by the different contexts. Table 1.1 (page 6) gives some sense of this diversity of research and the contexts of child rights.

This approach doesn't see 'child rights' as a monolithic one-size-fits-all phenomenon, with a basic set of commands that mean the same in every community and for every child irrespective of differences of age, gender, race, ability or sexuality. Rather, it sees child rights as something that has a variety of meanings: some work at international or national level, others at the local level of a particular school or health centre in a specific community which a child lives within. This book will identify and consider some of the questions arising from this perspective:

- What can be learnt from the many different ways that child rights are being *seen and interpreted*?
- What can we learn from the experiences of children and adults to date, now that *actual responses* in policy, law and practice have been attempted over the two decades since the UNCRC came into being?

In this way, the emphasis on the UNCRC is matched by a recognition of the many other initiatives, forces and ideas at work to champion, develop and test the ideas and practices in the lived experience of many communities and individuals.

Table 1.1 Research and examples of different contexts of child rights

Child rights research focus	Examples of research and enquiry	Discussion of specific focus in this book
Child poverty and child rights	Redmond, G. (2008) 'Child poverty and child rights: Edging towards a definition', *Journal of Children and Poverty*, 14(1), 63–82.	See pages 43 and 153
Child rights and war	Boyden, J. and De Berry, J. (2004) *Children and Youth on the Front Line: Ethnography, Armed Conflict, and Displacement*. Oxford: Berghan.	See pages 164–6 and 141–2
Child rights and sexual exploitation	Save the Children. (2006) *From Camp to Community: Liberia Study on Exploitation of Children*. Available online at www.savethechildren.org/ publications/liberia-exploitation-	See pages 62 and 144
Child rights and labour/work	Liebel, M. (2007) 'The New International Labour Organization (ILO) report on child labour – a success story, or the ILO still at a loss?' *Childhood*, 14(2), 279–84.	See pages 144–5
Child rights and inclusion in education for children with disabilities	Osler, A. and Osler, C. (2002) 'Inclusion, exclusion and children's rights: A case study of a student with Asperger syndrome', *Emotional and Behavioural Difficulties*, 7(1), 35–54	See pages 74 and 98–104

What do the different responses to the UNCRC reveal?

From another perspective, experience has revealed that concepts and practices related to child rights cannot, or should not, be accepted uncritically and that they may not be universally relevant. The following material contains a children and young person's perspective critiquing aspects of rights. It offers a sample of the UNICEF Summary of the UNCRC made for children, followed by a brief illustration from recent research in the United Kingdom made by children regarding their critique of the UNCRC and the UK government's response to the Convention. In addition, a sample of the European Union's material for children on a 'Strategy on the Rights of A Child' is followed by a brief illustration from Save the Children's research with children as a response to the EU Strategy.

Key points: perspectives on children's rights and children

Example 1: UNCRC excerpt and children's critique (UNICEF 'Children's Rights and Responsibilities')

Excerpt from UNICEF's summary of the UNCRC for children:

Article 1 Everyone under 18 years of age has all rights in this Convention.

Article 4 Governments should make these rights available to children.

Article 12 Children have the right to say what they think should happen, when adults are making decisions that affect them, and to have their opinions taken into account.

summary of A 12

Article 19 Governments should ensure that children are properly cared for, and protect them from violence, abuse and neglect by their parents, or anyone else who looks after them.

Article 28 All children and young people should have a right to a primary education, which should be free.

Article 31 All children have a right to relax and play, and to join in a wide range of activities.

If every child, regardless of their sex, ethnic origin, social status, language, age, nationality or religion has these rights, then they also have a responsibility to respect each other in a humane way.

(www.unicef.org.uk)

Example of research: 'what do they know?' CRAE Report on the UNCRC (Davey, 2008)

The Children's Rights Alliance for England's (CRAE) 'What Do They Know?' report (Davey, 2008) contained the views and experiences of children and young people relating to the implementation of the UN Committee on the Rights of the Child. The research was conducted by young people and involved 1,362 children and young people who filled in an online survey and 346 children and young people in focus group interviews. A delegation of 12 children and young people presented this

⇨

evidence directly to the UN Committee on the Rights of the Child in June 2008 at its pre-session working group in Geneva.

At present, it is clear that its as an editorial clarification (the UNCRC) implementation in England, both in legislation and practice, often leaves much to be desired. Children and young people, both in the online surveys and in the focus group interviews, gave very clear messages about what is important to them: knowing and being able to use their rights; being part of a family (meaning different things for different children); being respected, listened to and taken seriously; not being stereotyped; getting a good education; and living in a good area with a strong sense of community.

Listened to

The research revealed that very few children and young people knew what their rights were, and, of those who did, few knew how to act if rights were being denied or violated. The following gives brief illustrative examples of some of the key points raised, and of children and young people's specific comments:

In 2002 the UN Committee on the Rights of the Child recommended more effective mechanisms to ensure the systematic, meaningful and effective participation of all groups of children in society. In 2008, however, the UN Committee expressed disappointment that 'there has been little progress to enshrine Article 12 in education law and policy.' In our education survey, it was noted that although most schools operated a school council, only one in three children and young people (30%) felt that their views were always listened to by their school, and that primary schools were often better at involving children in decision-making than secondary schools.

They think because we're small and they're big

they know better . . . and they just treat us like we're

nothing, like we're just a puff of cloud or something.

(Child under-11; Davey, 2008, 15)

Although some children and young people were very aware of a growing change in attitudes towards hearing what they had to say, many felt that children and young people's participation in these exercises was often tokenistic:

tokenistic

Can't remember how many times I've been sat in the

chair, and someone's asked what do you not like about

Durham and nothing's changed.

(16- to 18-year-old)

Yeah, they ask you your say and then they say they're

listening, but then they don't take no notice of it so you

think, what's the point of saying it?

(Child in care; Davey, 2008, 16)

⇨

The research revealed that one of the changes identified by the respondents 'raised most often by younger children' was for the UK government to ban smacking and for support to be offered to parents to find alternative ways of raising children: 'that did not involve the use of physical force':

> *I would also stop smacking because if you do*
> *something violent to your child, they'll do it to their*
> *child, and it will go on which I think now would be*
> *bad, because then it will teach the whole world to*
> *smack and be violent.*
>
> (Child under-11)

Davey notes that the constant requests parallel demands from the UN Committee on the Rights of the Child in 1995, 2002 and 2008 for the UK government 'to remove the "reasonable chastisement/ punishment" defence and to prohibit all corporal punishment in the family' (Davey, 2008, 39).

Key points: perspectives on children's rights and children

Example 2: European Commission's Children's Rights Policy excerpt and children's critique

From 'You and the EU! The European Commission's Children's Rights Policy' (excerpt written for children):

> This paper is a summary of a 'communication' (an official paper) written by the European Commission which is called 'Towards an EU Strategy on the Rights of the Child.' It explains
>
> why a strategy (a plan) on children's rights is needed;
>
> what issues will be included in the strategy;
>
> how the European Commission will help turn the plan into action.
>
> Children's needs and children's rights cannot be separated. The respect and promotion of the rights of all children should go hand-in-hand with action to address their basic needs such as proper healthcare (good hospitals and medicines) or good schools and trained teachers. . . . It is therefore very important that a strategy or action plan is written to improve the situation of children around the world and to show how important children's rights are to the EU.

Objective One: To get the most out of existing activities and doing something about things that are urgent.

The Commission will continue its work on children's rights and continue to give money to projects promoting children's rights. At the same time it must do something about two things that need to be done urgently, which are explained below as 'urgent actions':

Urgent Actions:

1. To have a single telephone number (6-digit starting with 116) within the EU for child helplines and hotlines.
2. To launch an 'Action Plan on Children in Development Cooperation'; this plan will focus on children's needs in developing countries.

Objective Three: To mainstream children's rights in EU actions 'Mainstreaming' means to make sure that all EU policies, laws and actions respect children's rights and agree with EU and international law (such as the UN Convention on the Rights of the Child).

Objective Six: To produce an awareness-raising strategy for children on children's rights.

Awareness-raising is about people finding out more about an issue or subject.
An awareness-raising strategy with children on their rights is needed so that children can know more about their rights and how to use them.

The information discussed is available at www.crin.org/docs/FileManager/euronet/childfriendlyversion1317yrs.pdf

Example of research: Save the Children: You Could Always Begin by Listening to Us: A Consultation with Children on the EC Communication 'Towards an EU Strategy on the Rights of the Child' (2007)

This consultation involved questionnaires from over a 1,000 children from different member states within the EU. The following gives brief illustrative examples of some of the key points raised, and of children's and young people's specific comments:

Children were asked about what they identified as 'the most important issues affecting boys and girls in their country, why these issues were important and what needs to be done about them' (2007, 11).

In the consultation violence was identified 'as the single most important issue to address' (2007, 11).

Other issues were identified as. discrimination, social exclusion and racism, drugs, alcohol and smoking; poverty; the exploitation of children, protection of the environment and attitudes, information and support (2007, 12–15). Comments included:

It is useless to mainstream EU actions on children's rights when people are not really informed and educated about them (children's rights).

They could start by thinking of how they themselves would like to be heard if they were in our situation.

I think that the principal cause of adult misunderstanding is the absence of communication.

I would pretty much need a robot in the shape of an adult person, who can speak on my behalf. Then maybe someone would listen to what I have to say.

The EU can promote children's rights through mass media and the internet which are widely used to resolve daily problems. I think that in this case children's rights will be taken into consideration.

(2007, 17–18)

Reflections on the research

Activity 1
Review the research findings in relation to adult perspectives and child perspectives on rights described in this chapter: where can you identify parallels or tensions between adult and child perspectives? Why do you think these might be occurring?

Activity 2
In summarizing Sweden's ratification of the UNCRC Cohen, Moss, Petrie and Wallace cite the following measures taken by the Swedish government:

- The convention was to be incorporated into training and in-service training of professionals . . .
- All government decisions should be subject to child impact analyses so as to discover how any policy affected children
- The influence and participation of young people should be developed in social planning.

(2004, 142)

How do you see the ways in which the implementation of each of these measures might help address the criticisms (see pages 7–9) raised by research into UK children's and young people's experiences of the impact of the UNCRC? If implemented properly do you think they would, or would not, meet some of the criticisms?

Activity 3

Recent UK research concluded that 'More than four in five adults, especially those who were older and men without children or teenagers of their own, thought parents should be allowed to decide whether or not to smack their own children' (Madge, 2006, 72).

How do you see this finding in relation to the Key Points material above concerning the statements of child rights, children's views concerning the worth given to children's opinions, adult–child power dynamics and issues concerning protection and smacking?

Developing the above material, Chapters 2 and 3 will explore additional criticisms of the UNCRC that relate to the very ideas at the heart of the child rights philosophy and framework. Critiques relate to the way policies and practices have been formulated – from a macro – or international, level to the smaller scale of local polices and practices. Again, many years on from the UNCRC, it is important to ask what can be learned from these critiques? This book will introduce some of these criticisms and explore the questions they ask. In addition, the ideas of child rights have also been tested by beliefs, attitudes and the lived contact with individuals, communities, national and transnational forces that are directly or indirectly *opposed* to child rights. A key consideration here is whether we can see certain patterns or issues which are emerging? One reason to identify these is to ask what can be learned from the patterns in order to improve children's lives, and to see whether child rights as a concept, or as a set of emergent practices, needs rethinking?

These are the ideas that are central to the work of this book. We will establish some of the cornerstones of the initial child rights movement and give attention to key developments such as the UNCRC in Chapter 2. However, we will also look at different responses: critiques, challenges, the antagonisms to the ideas and practices of rights as well as the excellence of initiatives and drivers of change. In reviewing the contemporary situation in Chapters 2 and 3 our intention is to look at child rights to see what is *working* for children and those who live and work with them, as well as what needs *rethinking and changing* in order to see children's relationship with rights in new ways. The following sections introduce three key emergent issues within the contemporary response to rights:

- The rights dynamic
- A rights agenda
- Rights-informed approaches to relating to children

What issues are emerging in relation to rethinking children's rights?

Emerging issues: the rights dynamic

Positive developments following on from initiatives such as the UNCRC have included the many ways in which a *rights dynamic* has been created. This dynamic concerns the ways in which ideas about rights have acted as a catalyst or tinder within countries and societies. The impact has included laws or policies that have been created, or altered, as a response to the dynamic energy created by child rights ideas. As this book will illustrate, these are within different arenas and spaces: from the justice system to practices in play, education and medicine. This macro level of intervention then permeates through to the training of professionals and practices and to the micro level of work that relates to children in specific courts, schools or hospitals.

This *rights dynamic* also affects the ways debate and discussion occur. Laws, policies and practices are not fixed: how they are interpreted changes and develops, or specific laws and policies are created in response to new ideas about child rights. In this way, the concept and increased visibility of child rights is an emerging force that is used when international and national decisions are made in political arenas concerning the formation of laws or policies, for example. Looked at from this angle, the *child rights dynamic* provides a pressure for action enabling complex issues to be debated and understood. As Chapter 2 will discuss, this creates an impetus for change in particular, rights influenced, directions.

On a micro level, the *rights dynamic* can be seen as a lever to promote developments in local policy and practice. The *rights dynamic* here becomes a force within a setting or space where services are provided for children, or where children live. The energy created by knowledge of a rights perspective can affect how adults working with children see and review their work, for example, influencing how they create spaces and provision for children. Chapters 6 and 7 will look at how this dynamic, created by knowledge and promotion of rights, is present within children's experiences of families and in settings working with children.

As the book will reveal, the actual reflection and impact of children's rights in laws and policies is extremely varied. The level of awareness by children and adults alike is affected by a number of factors, including the ways that a society sees the position of children from political, economic, cultural and religious perspectives. In its 2008 Survey, based on responses of over a 1,000 children, the Children's Rights Alliance of England (CRAE) reported that, though under Article 42 of the UNCRC governments are obliged to widely disseminate information to children and young people about their rights, in England a 'majority of respondents said they knew very little about the UNCRC' and of those that had, '82% had not received this information through their school' (CRAE, 2008, 17–18).

Example of research: the rights dynamic at work – children's understandings of the UNCRC in Norway

A different situation is revealed by research undertaken in Norway (Sandbaek and Hafdis Einarsson, 2008) that looked at children's awareness of the UNCRC. This gives a relatively positive picture of children's awareness of their rights. A total of 1,274 children and young people from different regions within the country and from different backgrounds participated in the survey; 1,139 answered questionnaires, while 135 attended qualitative interviews. The respondents were asked whether they had heard of the convention and, if so, through which channel. Some questions concerned the content of the convention and whether the children thought it was important to them. A further question asked whether they believed they enjoyed rights in various everyday arenas such as their home, school, in leisure activities and in wider society. In sharp contrast to the Children's Rights Alliance of England's research findings, half of the Norwegian children had heard of the convention. There was some variation between the different regions of Norway, from 43 to 67 per cent. The report discusses the different ways in which children were aware, noting, for example, the respondents' references to a short version of the Convention in poster form issued by the Norwegian Ministry of Children and Equality:

> Two of the girls remembered seeing the poster and one said: '*Oh yes, that one! It's hanging in the classroom.*' The children at a day care centre . . . recalled what it said, that '*all children are entitled to have fun, to play, to have a place to live and to be fed.*' (Sandbaek and Hafdis Einarsson, 2008, 14)

One of the questions asked what the children thought the UNCRC was about. The research presented the following examples of children's perspectives based on the qualitative interviews and open boxes in the questionnaires given to pupils:

- I think it says that children in Norway should be happy at school and at home.
- I think it's about finding out what it's like for children in Norway, and it's about children's rights.
- That children should have all rights like going to school, having a home, being fed etc.
- I think it says that children should be happy and not afraid, but feel safe.
- Children's rights, that all children are entitled to decide and to be fed, go to school and to be loved.
- It's about children having rights to have a say and to have an opinion without being punished.
- It's about rules for children. It's sort of a book of the rights of children.
- I think it's about the rights of children in countries that are members of the UN

(Sandbaek and Hafdis Einarsson, 2008, 15)

Reflections on the research
Activity 1
Compare these comments from children with Table 2.2 (pages 43–4) in Chapter 2. It is possible to see the accuracy of many of the children's statements in relation to the UNCRC as well as children's own perceptions and language. The research report notes: 'These quotes show that while children linked the Convention to their own situation, several viewed it in a general perspective as something that applies to all children' (Sandbaek and Hafdis Einarsson, 2008, 15).

Activity 2
An earlier comment in this chapter discussed the importance of enabling children and adults to know about and to understand children's rights, arguing that 'the energy created by knowledge of a rights perspective can affect how adults working with children see and review their work, for example, influencing how they create spaces and provision for children.'

Compare the situation revealed by the research that showed English children were often unaware of rights, with the picture created by this research from Norway. How do you think *knowledge* of rights and the *impact* of rights are connected? What differences might there be for adults and children living and working together in a country where children knew very little about their rights and one in which the children were informed about child rights and their implications?

A rights dynamic, then, concerns how child rights as a concept can create an impetus for change, their presence acts as a catalyst, a meeting point and a pressure for action.

Key points: emerging issues – the rights dynamic

- The way 'child rights' as a concept has provided a language and framework to see children and childhood differently, and to draw attention to areas such as inequality and the need for radical changes.
- The dynamic energy created by child rights as a critical position to lobby for positive change in children's lives and the communities they are a part of.
- The impetus that the idea of child rights has had on macro levels of international and national government.
- The impact of child rights in rethinking and changing the day-to-day lives of children in the spaces they inhabit and in relation to the people and institutions they connect with.

Emerging issues: a rights agenda

If a *rights dynamic* concerns the ways child rights can animate and create an impetus for change the idea of a *rights agenda* concerns the pattern of issues which have emerged within the movements for change. This *child rights agenda* has fuelled much enquiry and research involving children and their lives. The particular focus of an agenda for action, change and research informed by rights varies according to local situations. These are two examples from Africa:

Child rights agenda: example 1
The first is from an organization that calls itself the 'Child Rights Agenda' (CRA) and sees rights in relation to all children having 'the inalienable rights

to grow up, free of poverty and hunger, to receive a quality education, to be protected from infectious and preventable diseases including HIV/AIDS, to grow up in a clean and healthy environment'.

The agenda here is translated into objectives. These are as follows:

Objectives:

1. To provide an end to all forms of discrimination and exclusion against children since every girl and boy is born free and equal in dignity using multidimensional approaches with the support and participation of various key stakeholders.

2. To promote the value of literacy between every child and their communities.
   (www.projects.tigweb.org/cranigeria)

Child rights agenda: example 2

The United Nations Office for the Coordination of Humanitarian Affairs reports on another perspective on child rights creating an agenda for action in West Africa. The summary describes a meeting co-ordinated by the regional office of Save the Children (SCF) Sweden and the Economic Community of West African States (ECOWAS) in 2002. Members of the armed forces of 13 West African countries and of non-governmental organizations ended a five-day meeting in Dakar, Senegal, with a call to reaffirm a commitment to 'international legal standards that protect children' affected by armed conflict:

A declaration approved by the participants in the meeting called on ECOWAS to ask member states to commit personnel, time and energy to mainstreaming children's rights and child protection (including the non-recruitment of children into armed forces, and responsible sexual behaviour towards children) in military training for all members of security forces. Another recommendation coming out of the Dakar meeting was for member states to ensure reporting mechanisms that allow military and civilian personnel to report abuses of children's rights during conflict.
(United Nations Office for the Coordination of Humanitarian Affairs, 2002)

This emerging *child rights agenda* is also repositioning children's experiences as worthy of consideration from a child's own perspective. As Chapter 4 will show, one example of such a shift has been from a position where interest chiefly lay in adults' perceptions, opinions or concerns regarding children's lives and experiences, to one that is more concerned with acting from a position informed by children's own perspectives. This idea often uses the metaphor of children's voice. It involves work whereby children are given tools to examine and express their ideas and opinions. An example of this is children being given access to decision-making processes such as meetings or committees. Another example involves decision-making processes using materials that enable children to understand, communicate or take part. This aspect of the child rights agenda often demands children's <u>involvement</u> in decision making and in the <u>implementation</u> of their ideas within areas such as service provision. These aspects of this agenda will be described further in Chapter 7. This shift has seen the *child rights agenda* to be one that is led by children's own perceptions of child rights and by children's ideas about changes needed in their lives. Originally, much of the impetus for change, the perspectives on what changes needed to be made, how change was progressing and the analysis of discoveries and barriers to rights-based actions were mostly, or completely, based on the opinions and ideas of adults. The examples of research in Chapter 4 illustrate that a part of the difference resulting from the *child rights agenda* involves the presence of children's own perceptions, experiences and demands within the forces that create and affect their worlds.

In her paper on 'Social Inclusion as Solidarity: Rethinking the Child Rights Agenda' Bach (2002) summarizes a theme present within a number of commentators on emergent themes in the response to child rights: the importance of connecting an agenda that emphasizes rights with a commitment to challenging social exclusion.

> Calls for inclusion as valued recognition are growing as the dilemma of the 'rights revolution' becomes clear – a context where rights are expanded and exclusion is entrenched. A social inclusion agenda could address this dilemma by promoting social solidarity across expanding social, ethnic and cultural differences that increasingly characterize and divide so many societies, often in destructive ways. Policy analysis should reveal ways that social, economic and political arrangements systematically undermine social solidarity by devaluing certain people and groups, even though their rights are assured (Bach, 2002, 4).

The key point she is making concerns the need to ensure that rights do not become an isolated arena, that the complex forces at work that exclude, silence and disenfranchise children are recognized and addressed. The child rights agenda is one that needs to engage with areas of 'social, economic and political' concerns in a way that promotes inclusion and equity.

Emerging issues: rights-informed approaches to relating to children

A key element of the emergent rights agenda is enabling a rethinking of the way *relationships* are created. This includes the ways in which organizations that govern, or that provide services, form a relationship with children. This book will focus especially on this as a key issue within the ways in which rights are affecting children's lives. This can involve a *child rights-informed approach* to how policies are created, and a *rights-informed approach* within the policies made that relate to how workers conduct interactions with children. The former might involve children in the creation of a setting's policies, the latter might concern the way adults engage with children in areas such as choice or involvement in decision making within everyday contact.

This connects with an important aspect of the ways in which the rights dynamic has begun to affect children's lives: it is enabling children to be seen and to be treated differently by adults. It is part of shifts in the ways children and young people see themselves, their relationships with each other, the adults they encounter and broader organizations that connect with their lives, such as national or local government. A theme within this shift has concerned children's representation of themselves, the empowerment of children and the valuing of children's perspectives on a range of issues. It emphasizes and recognizes the ways that children can actively take part in areas such as decision making and recognizes children's, autonomy and capacity.

A number of ways of working have become allied with this change. On the one hand, the influence of the philosophy and concepts of children's rights can be seen to be allied with the emergence of the new sociology of childhood. This is typified by emphasis on children as active, engaged agents in their own lives, challenging former stereotypes that saw children as passive or incapable. One of the forms this has taken, and a framework that runs through this book's consideration of rights, can be seen as *rights-informed ways of relating to children*. The following key points notes some ways that will be explored within this book and which research is telling us are becoming used in many societies:

Key points: rights-informed ways of relating to children

- Ways of involving children in decisions about their bodies, spaces and futures.
- Way of perceiving children's lives and experiences from a child's perspective rather than from the perspective of adult ideas and opinions about what children see, want or need.
- Specific services that are designed with children in mind rather that adult services with no, or little, adaptation for children.

- Spaces designed and created for children with input into the design, regulation or use of those spaces by children.
- Looking to see how children can be seen and engaged with as active, capable and as experts in their own lives.
- Changing adult roles and relationships with children in services and provision that try to address inequalities.
- Emphasizing child-orientated ways of participating or communicating, such as play.
- Identifying and addressing the particular ways in which social divisions within society concerning areas such as poverty, race, gender, disability and sexuality affect children, rather than seeing their impact on children's lives as identical to their impact on adults.
- Enquiry through research into children's experiences and ideas about a part of their lives or service.
- Reviewing the nature and role of policy and practice and rewriting documents and guidelines from a rights perspective.
- Changing decision-making processes to include children in decision about themselves, events or issues that affect them or within organizations that work for or with them.
- The role of advocacy within representation of children's views, opinions and decisions.

An example of the impact of the ideas of *rights-informed ways of relating to children* is a training pack funded by the UK government's Department for Children, Schools and Families called 'Ready Steady Change'. It contains two sets of materials – one for children and young people to increase their skills, knowledge and confidence in effective participation in decision making, and the other for those working with children and young people. The following sample of the stated beliefs of the training are an example of how the rights agenda is expressed in a reconfiguring of child–adult relationships.

- Children and young people have equal worth to adults.
- Children and young people have the right to be involved in all decision-making that affects them.
- Everyone that works with children and young people has a responsibility to encourage and support their active involvement in decision making.
- A commitment to children's human rights is key to achieving improved outcomes for children and young people.

(Ready Steady Change, CRAE/Department for Children, Schools and Families).

The rethinking of relationships, of which this is an example, has been manifested in new structures and bodies, reflecting a rights approach to the creation of new spaces for children to participate in. As Pain says, 'there are many . . . spaces and avenues of power where children and young people are denied access or a voice' (2000, 151). The emergence of new spaces marks a shift in a variety of attempts to respond to the rights agenda's demands of participation. The following table samples some of these new spaces which are discussed later in this book.

Key points: rights-informed new spaces

In local and national government

Children's parliaments or councils

See page 127

In law

The ways in which a child rights approach can be used to reassess areas such as youth justice and the way the law features in children's lives

See pages 175–8

Early years and education

Representation of children on decision making or governing bodies such as schools councils

Seeing educational settings and practices as spaces to implement and interpret children's rights

See pages 96–8 and 117–19

In hospitals and social care

Provision that is created to serve children in the creation of places and linked practices that are especially suited to children's use of health and social care services

See pages 129-31

A further examination of material involving rethinking children's rights and the idea of 'rights-informed ways of relating to children' can be found on pages 75–7, in relation to new ideas about children's consent.

How can negative responses to the rights agenda be used to help rethink children's rights?

Other responses to the child rights dynamic and agenda are less positive. As this book will show, in thinking about the development and implementation of a rights agenda a constant series of 'negative' themes, or problems, emerge. By identifying the ways in which they have manifested themselves it can help clarify how areas need to change – both at a macro and micro level. Some of the key issues which feature in this book concern are summarized below:

Key points: children's rights – problems and challenges

- Adult power used to prioritize the needs of adults, rather than those of children, in thinking about and taking action in relation to, child rights.
- Countries separating children into those who are 'worthy' of rights, and those who are not
- separating rights off from other processes, such as poverty or racism, that have a negative effect on children and the families and communities they live in.
- Entrenched customs and practices that resist changes that would benefit children
- The creation of the appearance of responding to children's rights – a 'rights veneer' but, in reality, making no real change or having little real impact on children's lives.

Emerging issues: a divided response

One kind of response can be summarized as a *divided response* to rights. Here adults separate off some children as worthy of a particular right, but see others as not worthy of the same rights. Hence, this is where rights are seen to be applicable to some children, but not to others. This is not to deny that in some spheres it is appropriate to make certain rights available to children based on their age or maturity. The Children's Rights Alliance for England, for example, draws attention to such differences when it talks about the differences between *voting* rights and *protective* rights:

> While CRAE strongly supports the extension of voting rights to 16 and 17-year-olds, this must not be confused with debates about 'age of majority'. There are a whole range of protective rights that 16 and 17-year-olds have, within domestic and international laws, related to child abuse, labour, involvement in war and

juvenile justice, for example. These rights recognize the difficult circumstances and challenges facing many teenagers, not connected to their capacity as individual people to vote.

(2000, 15)

The idea of a divided response becomes problematic when it concerns situations where rights are not given to some children or are removed. The removal of rights in this context is seen to be based on adult opinions or prejudices about the way children can, or should, live their lives, and where these opinions are not rooted in any evidence of benefit to children and/or primarily serve adult interests. Chapter 3, for example, looks at the ways in which the UK has *deliberately* maintained an opt out to allow it to deny children their rights. Chapter 4 looks at issues concerning the ways in which divisions based on adult stereotypes of age and competency are being challenged by new research into the capabilities and rights of children:

Extract from Chapter 3

For many years the UK government has *deliberately* retained an opt-out of the UNCRC. This opt-out allows child migrants and asylum seekers to be locked up without judicial scrutiny. So, whereas the UNCRC obliges nations to place the 'best interests' of a child first, the opt-out meant that the UK government did not need to apply it to these children. Therefore, officials could lock them up, sometimes for weeks or months pending deportation. . . . Following an inspection in 2008, HM Inspectorate of Prisons, for example, said that children were detained for too long and were left distressed and scared at the Yarl's Wood Centre in Bedfordshire.

Extract from Chapter 4

The tendency has been to link the worth and validity of a child's voice to adult opinions about appropriate 'levels' of competency and capability. This has often involved drawing broad lines about competency based on factors such as age. The idea being that a child becomes competent in a variety of areas at a certain age. Current thinking, research and areas of practice are questioning this.

Emerging issues: tensions, spaces, relationships

A tension exists between the different spaces and relationships within which children live their lives. One of this book's key themes concerns the tensions between children's experiences of spaces where rights-informed policies and laws operate and where they do not. This is a complex arena, as it concerns what can, and cannot, be governed by state law and policy. Aspects of children's home life is one example of this: how are children's rights present within the spaces of their home and in their family relationships?

Henricson and Bainham (2005, 81), for example, have summarized the kinds of tensions present within these different relationships and spaces. In discussing the rights of parents and the rights of children, they illustrate an example of this kind of tension. They argue that the overall situation is one where human rights commitments

> require the government to formulate policies that take account of the rights and needs of children and parents, but these needs are often competing.

They illustrate this by drawing attention to tensions between the interests of children, their families and the society they live within:

> In the context of the CRC, the age of criminal responsibility for children is too low (set at 10 in England and Wales). . . . On the other hand, the introduction and extension of Parenting Orders, which reinforce parents' responsibilities for controlling their children's behaviour up to the age of 16, do not take account of the degree of independence of this age group.

Another example of their analysis uses the idea of tensions between different interest groups in the spaces of education and justice:

> children's rights receive little recognition in the education arena. Parents' rights continue to be the dominant influence. Children, and in particular, young people, have little say over the choice of school, attendance, withdrawal from sex and religious education, and issues of discipline. Recent youth justice measures, such as Anti-Social Behaviour Orders and Parenting Orders, seek to promote the welfare of society; this risks being at the expense of children's and parent's rights.

This identifying of tensions between children's rights, parents' rights and society's 'welfare' is often referred to within the emerging response to child rights. Further examination of this and what it reveals about responses to children's rights can be found in Chapter 5:

Extract from Chapter 5

The UK government, for example, has increasingly emphasized the school as the physical location for a number of services for children and as a fulcrum for arenas of a child's life in areas such as health, welfare and play. Hence, the nature of the school space and the processes concerning schooling are key to any child. However, in the United Kingdom this crucial arena of a child's life is largely the domain of adult decision making, with children and their experience of the main space in their lives treated as the recipient of adult decisions. They are disenfranchised from the right to participate in most aspects of decision making within their main space in their life concerning the direction and regulation of educational experience and school life.

A further examination of material relating to rethinking children's rights and the impact of this 'divided response' to child rights and the UK's opt-out of the UNCRC can be found on pages 68–72.

The years since the UNCRC have seen tensions emerge regarding the relationships between other spaces in children's lives and how their lives are governed. An example of this include tension within the home space over the state's role and capacity to intervene regarding children's rights to protection and smacking. Such issues concerning differences, rights and children's spaces are considered in Chapter 6:

Extract from Chapter 6

The term 'abuse' within the family usually refers to physical and sexual abuse, but exactly what constitutes abuse is difficult to define. Instances of abuse within families are diagnosed as being pathological: not what 'normal families' engage in. One specific contentious area of potential abuse is smacking and, as this is still legal within the United Kingdom, it isn't seen as abnormal behaviour. Mason and Falloon question this adult-determined identification of abuse and researched the views of children in Australia on what they thought constituted abuse.

A further examination of material involving rethinking children's rights and issues concerning 'tensions, spaces, relationships' can be found in relation to children and surveillance on pages 78 and 146.

Emerging issues: a child rights veneer

Patterns within the emerging response have shown how it is possible for a *rights veneer* to be created. This rights veneer can be seen in many societies. As with the rights dynamic it occurs at different levels. The idea of a rights veneer is that structures or processes set in place give the *appearance* of engaging with a rights agenda, but do not *actually* do so. This may be deliberate, but often it is not a conscious intention, revealing just how difficult it can be to alter deep-seated and long-held views, attitudes and practices. On a large scale this could be concerning policies and laws that are not effectively enacted, on a small scale it might involve having a clear, rights-based position on paper and then in practice working in ways that ignore, or invalidate, the position. Chapter 5, for example, looks at research that challenges the rights veneer and rhetoric of the UK government's Every Child Matters in relation to the UN Committee on the Rights of the Child's critical review of their lack of progress;

Extract from Chapter 5

The treatment of children in terms of their rights to be involved in decision making in education varies. Some societies have developed a positive response to the rights dynamic, in areas such as children's involvement in decision making within education. Others, such as the United Kingdom have been criticized for their lack of progress by comparison, and the lack of structured, embedded engagement with children as decision makers. The UNCRC periodic review of the UK government notes, in 2002 for example, that obligations relating to Article 12 were not consistently incorporated in legislation. In terms of education, it criticized the UK government, saying that it needed to take further steps to promote, facilitate and monitor 'systematic, meaningful and effective participation of all groups of children in society, including in schools' (para 30) . . . in a way that 'reflects article 12 and respects children's rights to express their views and have them given due weight in all matters concerning their education'.

A further examination of material involving rethinking children's rights and the idea of a 'rights veneer' can be found in relation to research and children's participation on pages 73–4.

The presence of the UNCRC and negative responses

This chapter has introduced the key themes within this book. On the one hand, it has identified concepts and practices that have developed over the past two decades such as the *rights dynamic*, the emergence of a *rights agenda* and *rights-informed ways of relating to children*. It has also reviewed challenges and criticisms in relation to child rights.

Alston and Tobin (2005) comment on the development of the response to the UNCRC and its impact in ways that parallel the discussions in this chapter and in the book as a whole. In their review, they note the important ways in which the dynamic for change is both reflected in, and energized by, the UNCRC. They refer to positive elements and the enormous progress in children's lives, as well as the negative, persistent presence of violation, harm and oppression of children. This echoes commentators who have expressed grave concerns about the gap between rhetoric and reality. Alston and Tobin cite Moorehead's conclusions that the UNCRC has become 'something of a sham', primarily because it is violated 'systematically and contemptuously' by many countries, and that 'no countries violate it more energetically than those that were quickest to sign' (1997, pangaea.org/street_children/world/unconv3.htm).

More optimistically, they note the role of the UNCRC as an agent of change and that the presence of child rights is a crucial challenge in achieving urgently needed change:

> Increased government resistance to the scrutiny applied by the Committee on the Rights of the Child, is in many respects an indication that the process is starting to bite in the ways that it should. Efforts to reduce the age at which childhood is considered to end in relation to criminal responsibility or for other purposes, are in part a function of the pressures generated by the Convention to move to a standard benchmark of 18. Arguments designed to justify the detention of refugee children are being made with increasing vehemence, precisely because the Convention challenges such practices directly.
>
> (2005, 8)

This book reviews current thinking and research that is adding to that challenge in different spheres of children's lives.

Summary

This chapter has

- looked at the different ways in which societies see child rights,
- examined research into different responses to the UNCRC and the contemporary situation of child rights,

- reviewed different kinds of rights-informed ways of relating to children,
- emphasized the importance of connecting ideas and practices relating to children's rights with concepts such as social exclusion,
- explored how negative responses to the child rights dynamic be used to help rethink children's rights,
- looked at ideas of divided responses to child rights and the idea of a rights veneer.

Children's Rights: definitions and developments 2

Chapter Outline

Introduction and key questions   29
Is there a common understanding of the term 'right'?   30
What differences exist in relation to children's rights?   34
How can the history of children's rights help us understand
current issues?   40
How do ideas about adult–child relationships affect thinking about
children's rights?   48
What does research tell us about the state of children's rights
internationally and in the United Kingdom?   51
Summary   55
Further reading   56
Research details   56

Introduction and key questions

This chapter will outline some of the key definitions of children's rights, looking at international and national perspectives to help identify the ideas developed by the UNCRC and other initiatives. It includes a review of how the ideas and practices concerning children's rights have emerged as well as a summary of key points contained within the UNCRC. As Chapter 1 commented, the idea of 'Children's Rights' provokes many different kinds of response ranging from a wholehearted enthusiasm to a fear that children will run out of control. The response is likely to be based on the interpretation of two different but overlapping concepts: rights and childhood. This chapter examines these two concepts before going on to consider the issues for children and adults that arise from debates about rights and childhood. It attempts to answer the following questions:

Is there a common understanding of the term 'right'?
What differences exist in relation to children's rights?
How can the history of children's rights help us understand current issues?
How do ideas about adult–child relationships affect thinking about children's rights?
What does research tell us about the state of children's rights internationally and in the United Kingdom?

Is there a common understanding of the term 'right'?

The relatively recent popularity of human rights issues, particularly in the West, suggests that there is an inherent value in using a rights discourse and that there is some common understanding of concepts and values associated with the term 'right'. As will be seen later, the reality is much more complex and is bound up with the values that underpin the organization of societies and the power relationships within them. The position taken in this book is that the concept of rights is socially constructed in different ways and there are no 'natural' or absolute rights. However, different kinds of rights stem from different perceptions of the relationship between individuals and the rest of society. These differences are the basis of tensions and debates and the two main areas of rights, liberty rights and welfare rights, will be discussed here.

What are liberty rights?

In Europe and America the first real move towards consideration of rights came in opposition to power wielded by monarchs who were able to do anything they wanted and impose their will on any of their 'subjects'. The resulting ideas around 'the rights of man' were concerned with the rights of individuals to pursue their own lives without interference – liberty rights. This meant that no one should be compelled to do anything against his or her will and the state would only have the authority to intervene with the will of the people – essentially reducing the power that the state could have over what were now thought of as its 'citizens' rather than 'subjects'. Individuals would have the right to lead their lives as they wished: they would be autonomous human beings.

The legal systems developed identified the limits of individual freedom in cases where 'pursuing your own ends' would adversely affect others; for example, there would be laws against taking someone else's property or injuring others. These ideas were developed in France, by Voltaire, and, in America, by Franklin, Paine and Jefferson, and led to revolutions in both these countries and the emergence of the Bill of Rights in America. These 'liberal' ideas have developed in different ways over time, but the essence is the promotion of individual autonomy and independence with minimal state interference.

It may seem inconceivable now that these rights movements didn't include all sectors of society as having rights, but groups such as women and black people have had to fight for their rights during the last century. Mills (1859), while arguing for women's rights in the nineteenth century still argued that we should 'leave out of consideration those backward states of society in which the race itself may be considered as in its nonage' (1859, 23), a view that we would find totally unacceptable today, although another consideration that 'those who are still in a state to require being taken care of by others must be protected against their own actions' (1859, 22–3) is still a widely held opinion and is the basis for restricting children's liberty rights and, in some societies, the rights of women and other minority groups.

Key points: liberty rights

The UK Children's Commissioners' Report in 2008 identified a recent issue of liberty rights for children:

> we believe there has been an increase in discrimination against children as a whole. This is exemplified by the growing use of the 'Mosquito' device, a privately marketed product that issues a high frequency noise generally

only heard by those under the age of 25. The device is used to repel teenagers from public places and indiscriminately impacts on children's use and enjoyment of these spaces and highlights the intolerance of children in the UK. While the UK Government and devolved administrations have not endorsed their use, they have not taken any steps to ban them.

(UK Children's Commissioners' Report, 2008, 12)

Campaigners against this device see it as an infringement of the right of young people to gather together, while those using the device saw it as a means of supporting their right to carry out their business without intimidation from what they perceived as hostile groups.

In both these arguments the suggestion is that 'liberty rights' have been infringed: the rights of young people to gather together and the rights of shop owners to carry out their business.

How would you understand or resolve this conflict?

What are welfare rights?

Assumptions behind the idea of 'liberty rights' were that each individual would be responsible for him or herself, and his or her family, and that individual effort would result in a 'good life'. Great value was placed on individual autonomy and responsibility. This assumes that all individuals have the same start in life and have equal capacities to make a good life. Acceptance that this isn't the case, because some people are born into families that have more social and financial capital than others, led to discussion of another type of rights: welfare rights. These rights identify things that need to be in place to help everyone to make best use of their liberty rights. Areas within this framework include the following: a basic standard of living, health care, education, positive working conditions, rest and leisure, and participation in cultural life. While liberty rights call for an absence of state action, leaving individuals to their own autonomy, welfare rights call for state intervention to provide financial benefits, health care, education and so on for those who need them and to take action to ensure that the actions of employers, or others in powerful positions, do not endanger an individual's welfare rights. Consequently, there is a tension between these two types of rights, particularly because the state has to interfere with liberty rights through compelling people to pay taxes in order to fund welfare provision or to limit the actions of individuals and companies. In the instance of the sonic deterrent, for example, one of the arguments is concerned with the possible effects of the noise on the health of the young people involved and the need for state involvement to prevent this occurring. While liberty rights promote individual autonomy and responsibility, welfare rights stress the interdependence of individuals and shared responsibility for each other's welfare. Interestingly, the preconditions that Mills identified as being the basis for children (and others who need care) not being granted liberty rights are those that would mean they should be granted welfare rights; however, the extent to which these should be provided by the state rather than the family would be the focus for debate.

Key points: welfare rights

Waldfogel and Garnham (2008) reviewed the current policy on childcare and its effects on reducing child poverty. One of their findings was:

> The progress the government has made in extending paid maternity leave to nine months and eventually 12 months and also instituting some paid paternity leave, leaves a two-year gap between the end of paid maternity leave and the start of the entitlement to free part-time childcare when a child is age three. We recommend that the government undertake a focused consultation and review of policy options to address this gap.
>
> (2008, 24)

The effect of the two-year gap means that parents have to decide whether they can pay for child care while they go to work or look after the children themselves without any paid income. For families of low income and lone parents, however, either option is likely to leave the child in poverty and affect their welfare rights.

How might the welfare rights of these children be addressed?
How would this be funded?
What might families who have a good income and who pay for child care say about the welfare of these children?

What differences exist in relation to children's rights?

Rights and duties

While liberty rights and welfare rights prioritize different kinds of rights, and give different emphases to the roles of individuals and the community, they both focus on human beings as the central concern. Different societies and political systems deal with these tensions in different ways. Rights discourse has largely developed within the West with different societies giving more weight to one type of right than another; for example, socialist societies such as Venezuela tend to emphasize welfare rights, whereas liberal societies such as the United States tend to emphasize liberty rights. In contrast to the focus on humans as the centre of discussion, communities with strong religious beliefs or with strong hierarchical structures may have a different central focus: some divinity or supreme ruler. In these societies or communities, the Western concepts of welfare or liberty rights can be seen as subservient to the concept of duty: the duty of individuals to follow the teachings of the religion or the dictates of the leader of the hierarchy. The distinction between adults and children in this respect results in adults being further up the hierarchy. Children learn their overall duties from adults and may have specific duties to adults, for example, to obey their instructions and carry out specific tasks. Women may also be considered to hold a subservient position to men, with duties associated with that position. When this position is bound up with religion, and inequalities in status are seen as part of a 'natural' or 'god-given' order of duty, a rights discourse is very challenging.

Example of research: duties and rights

White (2007) analyses the *somaj* (local community) in Bangladesh where this concept of duty is identified through the common saying, 'In childhood girls are under the authority of their fathers; at marriage under the authority of their husbands; in old age under the authority of their sons' (2007, 512). She goes on to explain how these male 'guardians' are the full members of society and women and children only belong to the *somaj* by virtue of their relationship to them. Children's welfare is

---

protected by the guardian of the family, and the primary responsibility of the guardian is to 'make a person' by transforming the infant into a fully socialized human who fulfils the requirements of their specific gender role (2007, 513). Anyone who is excluded from the community, for example, through family breakdown, illegitimacy or by breaking rules, is without the protection and provision that the guardian is responsible for.

White concludes that

> there are strong contradictory and exclusionary, as well as solidary and inclusionary, aspects of the ways communities are imagined and conduct themselves in Bangladesh and these can impact badly on children who fall outside the charmed circle of 'guardianship', as well as meaning significant pressures on those who come within it.
>
> (2007, 518)

She points out that engaging in a rights discourse with these communities is meaningless, but to engage in a discourse based on the duties of guardians has enabled rights workers to improve conditions for children while being sensitive to cultural forms.

Reflections on the research

This research shows that though the concept of rights isn't universally accepted, the language of 'duty' and 'responsibility' can be used to engage those in powerful positions to consider how children's lives might be improved.

Activity

What are the positive 'solidary and inclusionary' features of 'guardianship'?

What might the 'significant pressures' be for those within the guardianship system?

What are the negative 'contradictory and exclusionary' aspects of 'guardianship'?

How do you think the use of a discourse around guardianship might improve the lives of excluded children and those within the community?

Ignatieff (2003) suggests that the strong criticism of a human rights approach from non-Western cultures is based upon the individualism that a rights discourse can promote and that this undermines religious or political values within certain cultures, communities or societies. This type of concern has also been expressed within Western societies by those who see the individualism and the increase in litigation around rights issues as undermining community spirit. A response has been to consider a Communitarian approach which emphasizes the interdependence of individuals. Communitarian principles, as explained by Etzioni (1995), seek to balance rights and responsibilities. However, getting agreement about what this balance might be is far from straightforward.

Key points: rights and duties

The language of rights is concerned with what an individual is entitled to have.

The language of duty is concerned with what an individual should do.

Rights are usually associated with responsibilities; for example, the right to privacy has an associated responsibility to respect other people's right to privacy.

Duties are usually associated with a moral commitment coming from a higher authority.

The concept of 'duty' is also associated with both welfare and liberty rights. The language of rights implies that there is a duty on others to ensure that rights are met. This duty can be of two kinds:

- 'Positive rights,' where there is a duty on the state or others to provide something that is necessary for an individual (usually associated with welfare rights), and
- 'Negative rights' where there is a duty *not* to interfere with what an individual wants to do (usually associated with liberty rights).

As individuals, rights holders have a duty to ensure that they don't interfere with the rights of others. This can become complex. For example, graffiti can not only be seen as an individual's right to free expression but also as an encroachment on the rest of society's rights to an unspoilt environment. Resolution of this conflict of rights would need discussion and compromise. If you consider these different points of view you will see how difficult it is to achieve a solution without further discussion of the boundaries of 'free expression' and what an 'unspoilt environment' might be. This type of problem leads to the need to establish rights within a legal framework. Conflicts are then resolved through the legal system.

Moral and legal rights

An important distinction needs to be made between moral rights and legal rights. While moral rights identify those things we feel should be rights, legal rights identify things that we are compelled to do, or not to do, by law. So, although we may say that someone has a right to food, water and shelter, unless there are legal imperatives that somebody has to provide these, the safeguarding of that right will depend on the voluntary actions of others.

Consideration of what constitutes a moral right varies from individual to individual and across societies and states. It is influenced by religion and culture and is likely to change over time and in different social and economic circumstances. However, in order for a moral right to become an enforceable legal right there needs to be some agreement that this is necessary, an agreement that is increasingly difficult as the number of people and the range of religions, cultures and circumstances is taken into account. Acknowledging the difficulty of agreement, Ignatieff (2003) suggests that, rather than seeing human rights as 'moral trumps', they should be considered as the basis for political discussion that takes into account political and social contexts, stressing the need for intercultural understanding.

Key points: moral and legal rights

Bisin (2007), reporting on work by UNICEF in Pakistan, identifies the very positive effects of improved water and sanitation facilities for school children. Prior to the work done by UNICEF, children had to walk for half an hour to get water from a stream and the older children collected water for the whole school. In the absence of any form of sanitation children defecated in the fields. The provision of a water tank and tap and latrines has not only decreased the health hazards to the children but also the time and attention they can give to their education. In this case, the water that is so important to the lives of these children and which, in the West, we take for granted, was provided by UNICEF, a voluntary organization. Due to a number of factors, including its economic situation, Pakistan is unable to make this provision for all its inhabitants.

If such basic provision is a 'right' who has the duty to ensure that this happens? Should it be left to voluntary organizations that are funded by voluntary contributions, or do richer states have a duty to make provision?

Could this be something that is enforced through a legal system or would it rely on a moral commitment?

This section has outlined two main types of rights: liberty rights and welfare rights. It has identified tensions related to these rights

between autonomy and the interdependence of individuals on each other,
between the provision of welfare rights and the maintenance of individual liberty
rights, and
between a rights discourse and a discourse based on duty.

These are summarized in Table 2.1.

Table 2.1 Rights, duties and different kinds of society

	Liberty rights	Welfare rights	Duties rather than rights
Examples of coverage of rights	Rights to life, liberty and property; freedom of thought, conscience and religion; rights to vote and take part in collective decision making.	Rights to an adequate standard of living, education, positive working conditions, rest and leisure and participation in cultural life.	Duties to others or to a deity are emphasized on the basis of tradition or religion.
View of society and the kinds of relationships that are implied	Liberal democracy Collection of autonomous individuals, each striving for the best for themselves. They may support others, who can't support themselves, through charitable endeavours but this would be a choice not an imposition.	Collectivism Interdependent individuals who work for and benefit from each other. All members of society are regarded as equal.	Individuals are subservient to a higher authority based on tradition or religion. Relationships between individuals are based on the tenets of the underlying belief. This may be hierarchical with those having the greatest knowledge and understanding of the belief system having the most power.
Role of the state	Minimal role to ensure safety of citizens from outside threats and to resolve disputes. Otherwise there is a requirement for the state not to interfere.	Strong role to ensure all citizens are provided for by sharing resources and contribute by fulfilling the required roles or No state as communities develop their own support systems.	Strong role in ensuring duties are carried out.
Associated values	Individual autonomy, tolerance, individual responsibility.	Equality, sharing and cooperation.	Morality on the basis of belief system.

Example of research: differences and rights

Penn (2001) researched the lives of children in Outer Mongolia, a traditional pastoral community that, since the break-up of the USSR, has moved from a collectivist political system to a more liberal democracy. Penn reports on research by Madsen who spoke to some children about their experience of this change. Under the communist regime everyone had been educated and had full health care but, under the new political system, these had to be paid for. Their responses illustrate the tensions between individual and society, rights and responsibilities and welfare and liberty rights:

> When there is a market economy there is also democracy. I read that in the paper. It is us who are going to decide. But we can't decide very much if we don't know what to decide about. That's why education is so important. . . . Lots of pupils have dropped out of school. There was one boy who was very clever but his family decided that he had to tend the animals. . . . I think it's very unfair, it's very, very bad for the children of our country.

> I have read a lot in the papers about what happened in Mongolia and in my society after the upheavals of 1989. Before there was political oppression in our country – I know that now but I didn't know it before. Now we are free – but the prices are so high that people became poor. That is because we have a market economy. . . . We are a little people. If we don't develop our production we will disappear as a people. . . . There are many people in the streets who are very drunk. It wasn't like that before and it makes me afraid.

Reflections on the research

The change in political system has brought about an increase in liberty rights with people having the opportunity to take part in decisions that are made by the state, but associated with this, individuals are expected to be able to take responsibility for their own welfare and that of their family.

Activity
Think about

- the welfare rights that were provided by the communist state,
- the liberty rights provided by the liberal democracy,
- what this young person identifies as necessary to make use of his liberty rights,
- how this might be provided,
- how the change might have affected adults as well as children and how they might perceive the change.

How can the history of children's rights help us understand current issues?

Are children's rights the same as human rights?

The current position of children's rights is a result of international debates about human rights and children's rights which have largely taken place in parallel. The changes over time reflect changes in thinking about liberty rights, welfare rights and who should have access to rights: children being a group that was considered to have special consideration. Earlier discussion referred to the fight that women and black people had during the twentieth century in order to obtain the vote. This is indicative of the way that liberty rights have largely been determined by the most powerful in the community: white males. While in democratic countries liberty rights are granted to all adults, in reality minority groups are still unlikely to be able to take full advantage of these rights either because they don't have the benefit of welfare rights that support access to liberty rights or because they are deemed to be inferior in some way.

The tensions around rights identified in the previous sections are unresolved and are apparent in debates at international, national and local levels. The origins of international human rights documents, such as the UNCRC, are often attempts to address the circumstances of the powerless to ensure that their voices are heard and issues such as exploitation, torture and discrimination are addressed. In parallel to human rights conventions, there have been conventions solely concerned with children's rights. In fact, the earliest convention focused on the rights of children.

Key ideas: the early stages of children's rights

Eglantyne Jebb, founder of Save the Children proposed the first five principles of the 1923 Convention of the Rights of the Child (Jebb, 1923):

1. The child must be given the means requisite for its normal development, both materially and spiritually.
2. The child that is hungry must be fed, the child that is sick must be helped, the child that is backward must be helped, the delinquent child must be reclaimed and the orphan and the waif must be sheltered and succoured.

---

3. The child must be the first to receive relief in times of distress.
4. The child must be put in a position to earn a livelihood and must be protected against every form of exploitation.
5. The child must be brought up in the consciousness that its talents must be devoted to the service of its fellow men.

An additional two points were added after the Second World War in 1948 with the realization that minority groups were in danger of persecution.

1. The child must be protected beyond and above all considerations of race, nationality or creed.
2. The child must be cared for with due respect for the family as an entity.

Activity

The language that this is written in and some of the ideas might seem strange in the twenty-first century but reflect the thinking of the time.

Go through each of the principles and think about

- the language that is used and how this might differ from the language used today,
- ideas about what is important for a child and whether these are still important today,
- the relationship between rights, responsibilities and duties.

These relatively simple formulations, in contrast to the 1989 Convention, stress the importance of welfare rights (Principles 1, 2, 3, 4 and the first of the 1948 additions) and establish the responsibilities children have to the rest of society (Principle 5). While Principle 4 suggests a degree of autonomy in being able to earn a livelihood the second of the 1948 additions stresses the importance of the child as part of a family, and none of the principles suggests that liberty rights are appropriate for children.

In contrast, the earliest attempt to identify a set of human rights rather than children's rights, contains both liberty and welfare rights. The title of the 1948 Universal Declaration of Human Rights (United Nations, 1948) suggests that there was universal agreement about its contents, but this wasn't the case. The rights outlined in this document consisted mainly of the liberty rights that individuals should have and also included welfare rights such as 'the right to work', 'rest and leisure', 'a standard of living adequate for the well being of himself and his family', and 'education'. The aim of the declaration was to encourage nations to commit themselves to attempting to achieve the identified rights. As such it was setting out a series of moral rights that it hoped would be incorporated into legal rights by individual nation states. Objections to the declaration illustrate some of the tensions identified earlier:

- Those from Islamic countries that were concerned that Islamic Shari'a law might be undermined,
- Those from libertarians who pointed to the conflict between liberty and welfare rights, because welfare rights have to be paid for, and this intrudes into the liberty rights of individuals being able to use their money as they wish.

The lack of international agreement led to a more limited 1950 European Convention on Human Rights (Council of Europe, 1950) that sought to identify a set of rights that would be legally binding across the nation states within the Council of Europe. Interestingly, given the objections to the Universal Declaration of Human Rights, the contents are mainly negative rights that prevent the state from interfering with individual liberty rights, and there is little reference to welfare rights. Individual member states ratified the convention (but could adapt some protocols to fit their individual circumstances) and ensured that their laws took account of the convention. Any individual within a state, after pursuing his or her case to the highest level within his or her own country, is able to appeal to the European Court of Human Rights. The United Kingdom developed the 1998 Human Rights Act in order to ensure that legislation took account of the Convention.

The 1989 United Nations Convention on the Rights of the Child (UNCRC) is an attempt to identify what the basis of children's rights should be in what is currently an adult-centred world. It argues for children's rights to be specifically identified, even though children are implicitly, and sometimes explicitly, included in Human Rights conventions and legislation. The Children's Rights Alliance points out that while there might be compassion for the plight of children in difficult situations, without a rights emphasis, it would be left to charity initiatives to address these difficulties. Having a convention focusing on children's specific rights would raise awareness and raise their political profile. Table 2.2 shows not only how the 1989 Convention on the Rights of the Child has some similarities with the European Convention on Human Rights but also where there are rights that are specific to children and some human rights that aren't considered to be relevant to children. The possible reasons for these differences will be considered later in the chapter.

Table 2.2 Children's rights and human rights (adapted from simplified versions of the conventions by The Children's Rights Alliance)

UN Convention on the Rights of the Child	European Human Rights
Article 1 The Convention applies to everyone aged 17 or under.	
Article 2 All the rights in this Convention apply to all children and young people without any discrimination.	Article 14 All the rights in the Convention apply to all people without discrimination
Article 3 Adults should always try to do what is best for children and young people.	
Article 4 Governments must do all they can to make sure children's and young people human rights are upheld.	
Article 5 Parents can give children and young people advice and help about children's rights.	
Article 6 The right to life	Article 2 The right to life
Articles 7 and 8 The right to a name and a nationality and the right to be cared for by both parents	Article 8 The right to respect for private and family life, home and correspondence
Article 9 If a court is thinking about who a child or young person should live with, everyone affected by the decision should get the chance to be heard – including the child Every child and young person has the right to keep in regular contact with both parents, so long as this is the best thing for the young person.	
Articles 10 and 11 The right to keep in touch with parents who live in another country.	
Article 12 The right to express his or her views freely and these must be given 'due weight' depending on his or her age and maturity.	
Article 13 The right to freedom of expression, including the right to all kinds of information and ideas	Article 10 The right to freedom of expression
Article 14 The right to freedom of thought, conscience and religion	Article 9 The right to freedom of thought, conscience and religion

(Continued)

Table 2.2 (Cont'd)

UN Convention on the Rights of the Child	European Human Rights
Article 15 The right to meet people and to gather in public	Article 11 The right to freedom of assembly and association
Article 16 The right to privacy	
Article 17 The right to information and protection from harmful information and materials.	
Article 18 Parents must always do what is best for children and young people and governments should help them	
Article 19 The right to protection from all forms of violence, abuse, neglect and mistreatment.	
Article 20 The right to special protection and help when separated from parents.	
Article 21 The child's best interests must be the top priority in adoption	
Article 22 The right to protection and humanitarian help for children and young people who are refugees, or who are trying to be accepted as refugees	
Article 23 The right to a full life and to active participation in the community for disabled children and young people.	
Article 24 The right to the best possible health and health services.	Article 13 The right to an effective remedy
Article 25 Children and young people who are in care or live away from home for health reasons have the right to have their care reviewed regularly.	
Article 26 The right to have enough money.	
Article 27 The right to a standard of living that helps them develop fully	
Articles 28 and 29 The right to education	
Article 30 The right to enjoy their own culture, religion and language	

Table 2.2 (Cont'd)

UN Convention on the Rights of the Child	European Human Rights
Article 31 The right to rest, play and leisure.	
Article 32 The right to be protected from harmful work and economic exploitation	
Article 33 The right to be protected from illegal drugs	
Article 34 The right to protection from sexual exploitation (including prostitution) and sexual abuse	
Article 35 The right to protection from being taken away, sold or trafficked	**Article 4** The right to protection from slavery
Article 36 The right to protection from all other exploitation	
Article 37 The right to protection from torture or other cruel, inhuman or degrading treatment or punishment	**Article 3** The right to protection from torture or inhuman or degrading treatment or punishment
Article 38 Governments must do everything to stop children under 15 from being involved directly in a war and care for children who are affected by war	
Article 39 Governments must give good support to children and young people who have been hurt, abused or exploited	
Article 40 Every child or young person accused, or convicted, of committing a crime must be treated with respect and in a way that helps them to respect the human rights of others	**Article 6** The right to a fair trial, including the child's right to be informed promptly, in a language he or she understands, of the alleged offence and to have an interpreter in court if he or she cannot understand or speak the language used in court. Restrictions on reporting can be applied to protect the interests of children
Article 42 The right to information about the convention	
	Article 5 The right to liberty and security
	Article 7 No one can be punished for an act that was not a criminal offence when it was carried out
	Article 12 Right to marry

What ideas underpin the 1989 Convention on the Rights of the Child?

Key points: the 1989 United Nation Convention on the Rights of the Child

The 1989 Convention on the Rights of the Child consists of 54 articles; 41 of these articles identify the human rights to be respected and protected for every child under the age of 18 years and require that these rights are implemented in the light of the Convention's guiding principles:

- Non-discrimination (Article 2),
- The best interests of the child as the primary consideration (Article 3),
- Survival and development of all children (Article 6),
- Participation of children in decisions that affect them: 'the views of the child being given due weight in accordance with the age and maturity of the child' (Article 12).

The 41 articles that identify children's rights are often referred to in three main groups: the three Ps. These are as follows:

- Provision to ensure children's survival and development (welfare rights),
- Protection from abuse and exploitation (welfare rights),
- Participation in decision making (liberty rights).

However, it is clear from the convention that rights should not be thought of individually but as a whole.

Table 2.3 takes key elements from each of the guiding principles of the Convention (1989) and links them to the kinds of questions relating to rights that this book will explore.

In contrast to the European Convention on Human Rights both liberty and welfare rights are covered in the Convention, and they are largely positive rights, requiring the state to act to ensure that rights are met. However, without a legal basis they remain moral aspirations rather than enforceable rights. The 1989 Convention has been ratified by all but two countries (Somalia and the United States). Through ratification states are agreeing to ensure that their laws and policies take into account the articles within the convention. They accept their responsibilities for ensuring children's rights are met within the state and report to the UN on the progress that has been made on a regular basis. In 1991, through ratification of the treaty, the United Kingdom committed itself to ensuring that the principles of the

Table 2.3 UN Convention on the Rights of the Child – principles and questions

UN Convention on the Rights of the Child	Questions
Guiding principle: Non-discrimination Children must be treated without discrimination of any kind, irrespective of race, colour, sex, language, religion or other status (Article 2)	How does discrimination particularly affect children? How can discrimination against children be stopped by a rights perspective? (for further discussion see Chapter 3, pages 70–3; Chapter 4, pages 98–100; and Chapter 7, page 171)
Guiding principle: Best interests of the child In all actions concerning children, whether undertaken by public or private social welfare institutions, courts of law, administrative authorities or legislative bodies, the best interests of the child shall be a primary consideration (Article 3)	What does acting in the best interest of the child mean in relation to rights? What is the relationship between adults' perceptions of the best interests of children and children's own perceptions of their own best interests? (for further discussion see Chapter 2, page 51; Chapter 3, pages 70–3; and Chapter 7, pages 172–5)
Guiding principle: survival and development States recognize that every child has the right to life and that states shall ensure, to the maximum extent possible, the survival and development of each child (Article 6)	What forces affect children's survival and development? Are all states able to ensure the survival and development of each child? (for further discussion please see Chapter 2, pages 37–8, and Chapter 3, pages 77–9)
Guiding principle: participation States shall assure to the child who is capable of forming his or her own views the right to express those views freely in all matters affecting the child, the views of the child being given due weight in accordance with the age and maturity of the child The child shall, in particular, be provided with the opportunity to be heard in any judicial and administrative proceedings affecting the child, either directly, or through a representative or an appropriate body, in a manner consistent with the procedural rules of national law (Article 12)	How does society define when children are old or mature enough to express valid views? (for further discussion see Chapter 4, page 96) What is the relationship between adult attitudes and children's experiences of holding views, participating in decision making and having decisions listened to and acted on in relation to rights? (for further discussion, see Chapter 4, page 96) How are children being heard within arenas such as the justice and administrative systems that they encounter? (for further discussion see Chapter 4, pages 90–4)

UNCRC would be incorporated into UK law. However, unlike the European Convention on Human Rights, unless elements of the convention are incorporated into national law there is no legal basis for the rights and no means of appeal outside the country in question. While acknowledging these difficulties relating to the mechanisms for its implementation Bell et al. (1999) point to the positive processes of 'moral pressure, dialogue and co-operation' (1999, 28) that take place rather than 'strong enforcement mechanisms' and assert that the key factor in making progress is 'political will' within each state. They argue that this slow progress will be more effective in drawing all states into a meaningful debate. They point out that very different societies have ratified the convention and claim that, by stressing the fact that no society has fulfilled the aims of the convention, it isn't promoting a particular view of society: an approach in tune with Ignatieff's appeal to dialogue rather than 'moral trumps' as a means of effectively engaging with rights issues.

How do ideas about adult–child relationships affect thinking about children's rights?

Earlier sections have identified the debates that exist around general rights issues, but these are further complicated when we consider *children's rights*. This is because 'child' is another socially constructed concept that differs across time and culture. This gives rise to different ideas concerning

- the status of children, and
- how this impacts on the relationships between children and adults and the relationship of the state to children and their carers.

Alanen and Mayall (2001) argue that the concept of 'child' can only exist as a contrast to that of 'adult', so our notions about what being a child means are bound up with what we think being an adult means. The first problem with the concept of 'child' is that it covers a very wide age range, and different societies see the transition from 'child' to 'adult' occurring at different times. By grouping all humans under a given age together and identifying them as 'children', we are in danger of seeing them as a homogeneous group with common characteristics, which is patently not the case. The ways that adults and children relate to each other is affected by, and affects, the constructs that we have of children and adults. These change over time and across cultures and have become an interesting focus for study. One feature of the adult–child contrast is that childhood is often seen as a time of 'becoming': the end point is seen as achieving adulthood. Consequently <u>children are seen as lacking the competences associated with 'being an adult'</u>, and 'being an adult' is seen as being the ultimate in development. This is closely related to the liberal view of rights in that liberty rights are granted on the basis of independence, autonomy and competence. Challenges to this 'all or nothing' contrast point to the

being an adult is the end point

- variability in adult competence and autonomy,
- competence of even very young children in many spheres,
- questionable value attributed to rational autonomy as the desirable end product.

These challenges are providing a way of rethinking the relationships that might exist between children and adults and Table 2.4 illustrates the implications of different ways of thinking. There is some parallel here with the rights debates in emphasizing either autonomy or interdependence.

The kinds of thinking and approach to the relationships between children and adults represented by Table 2.4 represent challenges to the ways relationships have been conducted in many societies. The development of a rights agenda, or the rights dynamic discussed in Chapter 1, can be seen within the review of relationships in the table. This is resulting in a way of questioning how relationships are conceived of and conducted. Within the United Kingdom the emphasis in current policy such as Every Child Matters (DfES, 2004) is on protecting children. It stresses the vulnerability of children but is in danger of ignoring other positive attributes.

As discussed earlier, one of the problems identified with the Universal Declaration of Human Rights was the inclusion of welfare rights. Interestingly, this isn't the main focus for criticism of the concept of children's rights: here the arguments revolve around giving children liberty rights. This largely stems from the perceptions of children that exist. It might be argued that the inclusion of some liberty rights for children in the 1989 Convention reflects the changing perception of children, although Bell et al., reporting on the first ten years of the convention's life, consider that the convention not only reflects changing perceptions of children but has also supported that change. They identify changes in the perception of children and in the basis of adult intervention, as summarized in Table 2.5.

[Handwritten margin note: Summary of child as an active or passive recipient — participation v. protection]

Table 2.4 Rights, children and adults

View of the child	View of the adult	Child–adult relationship	Implications for rights
Someone who is • a passive recipient of adult protection and provision • lacking adult competences of rationality and agency • dependent on adults • in need of control	Someone who is • strong and capable and knows what is best • able to make rational decisions and take responsibility • independent	Unequal power relationship Adult as protector, provider and decision maker for the child. Child responds positively to adult control Where the child does not respond positively to adult control the relationship becomes one of challenge and conflict.	Emphasis on welfare rights but not liberty rights
Someone who is • an active participant in their family and immediate community • developing but is resilient with many strengths • economically dependent on others but also contributes to the family and community	Someone who is • an active participant in their family and immediate community • able to make rational decisions and take responsibility but also makes mistakes and has a lot to learn • economically independent but is also dependent on others socially and emotionally	A mutually respectful relationship with an appreciation of the strengths and weaknesses of each other Adult is sensitive to the growing capabilities of the child and supports and involves them in making decisions. Children are encouraged to contribute and take responsibility within the family and community	Welfare and liberty rights

Table 2.5 Perception of children pre- and post-1989 UN Convention on the Rights of the Child

	Pre-1989 Convention	Post-1989 Convention
Perception of children	• Incompetent • Dependent • Powerless • Politically silent	Emphasis on children's dignity, competence, resilience and right to have views heard
Basis of adult interventions	• Charity • Confused ideas of protection (of adults from children as well as the protection of children themselves) • Need to isolate children from the adult world • View that children should be seen and not heard	Children's organizations demanding to have a political voice

What does research tell us about the state of children's rights internationally and in the United Kingdom?

Research that involves children in identifying their concerns and issues in relation to specific rights can help us to consider the difficult balance that is needed between protecting children and promoting their interests, ideas about what 'in accordance with their age and maturity' and 'in the best interests of the child' might mean and how states have responded to the UNCRC principles.

Example of research: protecting children and promoting their best interests in the labour market

In the United Kingdom children over a certain age are allowed to undertake paid employment with the consent of their parents. The hours that they work and the type of employment they engage in are restricted by their age. Leonard (2004) investigated the views of 245 15-year-old children in Belfast on the relative involvement of parents and children in the decision of children to engage in paid employment and the kind of employment they engaged in. She found that over half (58%) felt that parents should be involved in the decision and that the decision shouldn't be made by the child on his or her own. However, 32% felt they should be able to make this decision without consulting their parents. The range of employment engaged in was also beyond that identified in law.

⇨

Interviews with children suggested a sophisticated understanding of working conditions and their own capabilities that challenged the idea that their parents would know what is best and that there needed to be restrictions on the type of employment. This is illustrated in the following responses:

> It is a matter of freedom of choice whether or not you work and people around the age of 15 should have enough sense to judge whether they are treated fairly by their employers.

> I think people under the age of 16 should make their own choices about the hours they work but they should know their rights so they can make a good choice.

> Young people working should not be treated as inferior in the workplace by adults doing the same job. Our rights should be the same and we should be treated the same.

> I think employers think we cannot be trusted until we are 16 or we cannot be dependable. Children should be able to work if they feel they are ready for it and not just because they happen to reach the age of 16.

Leonard concludes that current UK employment legislation hasn't incorporated the principles of the UNCRC because there is a tendency 'to highlight children's vulnerability and in the process render invisible the extent to which children's lack of civil status promotes their vulnerability' (p. 59).

Reflections on research

Although Leonard isn't suggesting that children alone should be able to make these important decisions, she is suggesting that the current legislation ignores their views completely and identifies their parents as those who will be able to determine what is in the child's best interests.

Activity

What sort of relationship between adults and children does the legislation suggest?

What would need to change to make the relationship one that is more in line with the UNCRC principles?

How do the comments of the young people involved in the research reflect a different view of 'the best interests of the child' and 'age and maturity' to the legal framework?

Small-scale research such as this can feed into evaluations of how well individual states are responding to the UNCRC, in order to evaluate its effectiveness on a wider scale.

Research into the implementation of the 1989 UNCRC was undertaken in 1999 and reported on by Bell for The Save the Children Alliance. The researchers focused on the achievements of the 25 countries that are part of the Alliance, and these are largely stable and economically developed. While pointing to many positive outcomes, the report identifies a number of issues that are fundamental to ensuring a positive impact for children, as shown in Table 2.6.

There are clear themes throughout these issues that reflect the questions we have been concerned with in this chapter:

- the lack of a common understanding of what we mean by children's rights,
- the tension between welfare rights and liberty rights (in this case protection and participation) influenced by the view of children within society,
- whether everyone has equal access to rights,
- ambivalence about the status of children and the relationship between children and adults,
- the need for welfare rights to be funded and the problems about who is responsible for this.

The earlier discussion of rights shows that getting a common understanding of rights in general hasn't been possible, so that when the added complexity of a lack of common understanding of 'child' is added, the possibility of getting agreement on children's rights seems impossible within one community, let alone universally. However, although agreement may be a very long way off, the willingness to engage in debate enables change to occur, perhaps slowly, but in a way that is embedded rather than the superficiality that comes with imposition. Ignatieff's plea of not taking the moral high ground when discussing rights seems to have been an effective strategy in the progress that has been made around the implementation of the UNCRC so far. By acknowledging that every state has issues, rather than setting up a league table of achievement, there is more scope for open debate and finding ways forward that take into account different cultural perspectives. This wouldn't mean taking a position of cultural relativity whereby 'anything goes' but would mean taking a position more inclined towards cultural sensitivity. What does seem to be important is that children are included in that debate.

Table 2.6 Issues from research

Issue	Observations
Ratification and reservations	There are still two states that haven't ratified the convention, and many of those that have ratified it have reservations relating to specified articles. This means that there is still a long way to go in terms of universal acceptance, let alone universal understanding
Awareness of rights	In the majority of countries there was a lack of awareness of children's rights and the implications of the UN Convention on the Rights of the Child (UNCRC) at all levels from offices with national government and local government down to children and those who care for them
Deepening commitment	Only Sweden has an explicit strategy for implementing the UNCRC
Tackling the political sensitivity of some areas	While action has been taken on areas where there isn't any challenge to the prevailing view of the child, other areas are more sensitive and haven't received attention: • freedom of information, association and religion – while protection has been addressed, enabling children to access information and make decisions has not been addressed • democratization of schooling • protecting children's rights within the family while respecting dignity, privacy and integrity • implementing the principle of discrimination – girls, children in institutions and on the streets, minorities, disabled children and those in poverty are still discriminated against in many ways
Mechanisms for research and reporting	Unless there are clear mechanisms for getting a clear picture of progress and issues it is difficult to hold states accountable. It is important that these mechanisms include the involvement of children
Resourcing and child-friendly economics	It is important to have transparency of where and how money is spent and how effective this is and support for poorer countries is addressed
Mainstreaming rights	Making clearer links between the UNCRC and Human Rights legislation
Children in conflict	This is an area where the convention needs to be strengthened to give greater protection to children, particularly child soldiers
Political will	All parts of society need to feel that implementation of the UNCRC has something to do with them including government structures, voluntary and private bodies, civil society and media

Activities
The following activities are designed to help reflect back on some of the key concerns over the chapter as a whole.

Chapter activity 1
Go back through the chapter and list points made about each of the following:

   Liberty Rights:
   Welfare Rights:

Chapter activity 2
Table 2.4 identifies the implications for child–adult relationships of the different ways we might think about children. Go back through the chapter and look at the examples of research. Identify:

   a. What kind of relationship is exemplified in each example?
   b. How the relationship might be different?

Chapter activity 3
The conclusion to the chapter suggests that

> a common understanding of rights in general hasn't been possible so when the added complexity of a lack of common understanding of 'child' is added the possibility of getting agreement on Children's Rights seems impossible within one community let alone universally.

(i) look back through the chapter and identify where differences in understanding are noted and consider the implications of each of these on children's lives
(ii) Discuss the ways in which (a) a common understanding across societies, cultures and nations would be something that can be viewed positively or negatively for children, and (b) the ways in which a diversity of understandings might be a positive or negative experience for children.

Summary

This chapter has

- identified the different understandings of the term 'right',
- examined the tensions that exist in relation to ideas about children's rights and their implementation,

- identified how the history and development of children's rights can help in understanding current issues,
- explored how ideas about adult–child relationships can affect thinking about children's rights,
- identified the ways in which research can help to review the state of children's rights internationally and within the United Kingdom.

Further reading

Archard, D. (1993) *Children: Rights and Childhood*. London: Routledge.
The first three chapters explain the relationship between different conceptions of children and the way child rights are interpreted.
Franklin, B. (2002) *The New Handbook of Children's Rights: Comparative Policy and Practice*. London: Routledge.
Chapter 1, 'Children's Rights and Media Wrongs', gives a very clear overview of issues around children's rights and other chapters look at these in more detail.

Research details

Example of research: duties and rights

In a peer-reviewed journal, White (2007) investigates the different images of children in Bangladesh and how they relate to different ways of 'imagining' the community. This is reflected in the culture of 'guardianship' that contrasts with the concept of 'rights'. The paper is largely conceptual but draws on pieces of ongoing research.

White, S. (2007) 'Children's rights and the imagination of community in Bangladesh', *Childhood*, 14, 505–20.

Example of research: differences and rights

Penn (2001) presents an analysis of the context of the lives of children in outer Mongolia based on her observations of children and children's own views as well as adult reminiscences and commentaries. She also draws on Mongolian statistics and reports from development agencies.

Penn, H. (2001) 'Culture and childhood in pastoralist communities: The example of outer Mongolia', in Alanen, L. and Mayall, B. (eds) *Conceptualizing Child-Adult Relations*. London: Routledge/ Falmer.

Example of research: protecting children and promoting their best interests in the labour market

In a peer-reviewed journal, Leonard (2004) examined children's attitudes regarding the right to work through focus group interviews with 94 young people from 12 schools and interviews with 15 working pupils.

Leonard, M. (2004) 'Children's views on children's right to work: Reflections from Belfast', *Childhood*, 11, 45–61.

Implementation of the 1989 UNCRC

Report commissioned by Save the Children Alliance that analyses progress reports from the 26 member countries to identify areas of success and issues for development.

Bell, B., Brett, R., Marcus, R. and Muscroft, S. (1999) *Children's Rights: Reality or Rhetoric? The UN Convention on the Rights of the Child: The First Ten Years*. London: Save the Children.

Part 2
An Interdisciplinary Review of Recent Research and Scholarship

Children's Rights: current tensions, debates and research

Chapter Outline

Introduction and key questions   61

What are current, emerging tensions and debates in relation to
children's rights?   62

What are some of the implications of these tensions?   66

What is research showing us about tensions and debates
concerning children's rights?   73

Summary   80

Further reading   81

Research details   81

Introduction and key questions

Sinclair (2004) has described the area of rights in relation to children as emerging from the convergence of new, and developing, ideas and debates from a number of different perspectives. These are identified by her as follows:

- the children's rights agenda;
- new paradigms within the social sciences that have increased our understanding of the child as a competent social actor, seeing their capacity to be commentators in their own lives and to be involved in decision making;
- pressure from children and young people, researchers, policy makers and practitioners working with children.

This chapter will review recent research and enquiry that can help to explore the developments in thinking and practice introduced in Chapters 1 and 2. The focus will be on the following:

What are current tensions and debates in relation to children's rights?
What are some of the implications of these tensions?
What is research showing us about tensions and debates concerning children's rights?

What are current, emerging tensions and debates in relation to children's rights?

Chapters 1 and 2 noted that it has become usual to divide the UN Convention into particular areas of concern: these are often identified in terms of liberty and welfare rights or of three kinds of rights: provision, protection and participation. However, others draw attention to different ways of critiquing and approaching the UNCRC in ways that can help illuminate aspects of child rights. Freeman (2000), for example, sees the UN Convention in terms of 'articulating' areas of rights in a particular way. These include 'general rights' – to life; freedom of expression, thought and religion; the right to information and privacy; and against being subjected to torture. Another area is seen to be rights requiring 'protective measures' such as those that protect children from economic and sexual exploitation, to prevent abuse and neglect. The UNCRC also can be seen to address the 'civil status' of children. This area includes the right to acquire nationality, to preserve one's identity, to remain with parents (unless the 'best interest' of the child indicates otherwise) and the right to be reunited with family. Rights are also seen to relate to what is described as special circumstances. These include children with disabilities, refugee or orphaned children and the concerns of minority children.

Other attention emphasizes *particular aspects* of the UNCRC. Some, for example, have argued that the UNCRC is distinguished from other rights-based initiatives in its attempt to implement policies through its inclusion of, and emphasis on, *participation* as a key cornerstone of change:

> Participation is the keystone of the arch that is the UNCRC. Without the active participation of children and young people in the promotion of their rights to a good childhood, none will be achieved effectively.
>
> (Badham quoted in Willow, 2002, vi)

This way of analysing the UN Convention on the Rights of the Child, sees participation as its heart and is summarized by Hill and Tisdall as the view that children are active, engaged participants in their lives, and, in society, as 'social actors with their own views and goals, and not just objects or problems' (1997, 28). They quote a child asserting that children should have 'the rights of agency: to take part in family decisions, rights to make our own decisions about our future, rights to live our own life and not what our parents want us to do, the right to our own opinion' (CRDU, 1994, 24). As outlined in Chapter 2, the change here involves seeing children in their own right and as having rights, not as proto-adults, or as the property of parents. However, issues regarding participation are subject to different interpretations and tensions around childhood and society. Authors such as Freeman note that in the UNCRC's development there were 'stumbling blocks' in relation to the formulation of child rights – in areas such as participation and freedom of thought, conscience and religion. This analysis of a developmental perspective on the Convention can help to understand and illustrate some of the tensions within the UNCRC referred to in Chapters 1 and 2. Freeman comments, for example, that 'Islamic nations particularly were concerned with the implications of this. Inter-country adoption offended . . . Latin American countries' (2000, 278). Issues such as the rights of the unborn child, female genital mutilation and differences on whether children should have 'duties' were also noted by him as contentious issues which were not resolved in relation to the final form that the UNCRC took. 'Duty' as a concept found its way into the Charter on the Rights and Welfare of the African Child, but was excluded from the UN Convention. He points to these areas as ones of eventual compromise, for example on religion, 'by the adoption of a minimal text' (2000, 278). Freeman concludes that whether these compromised positions are 'necessarily good' for children can be contested.

Other perspectives on the UNCRC have argued that a rights approach in itself is inadequate. Bach summarizes this approach well:

> Whether the source of exclusion is poverty, racism, fear of differences or lack of political clout, the consequences are the same: a lack of recognition and accept-ance; powerlessness and 'voicelessness'; economic vulnerability; and, diminished life experiences and limited life prospects. For society as a whole, the social exclu-sion of individuals and groups can become a major threat to social cohesion and economic prosperity. A rights-based approach is inadequate to address the per-sonal and systemic exclusions experienced by children and adults. People with disabilities are leading the way in calling for approaches based on social inclusion and valued recognition to deliver what human rights claims alone cannot.
>
> (Bach, 2002, x)

Here the interrelationship between a number of different perspectives are emphasized. The central tenet of this critique is that rights and processes of social exclusion need to be addressed within different arenas of children's lives in ways that acknowledge the interconnectedness of rights, powerlessness, economic vulnerability and a lack of political acknowledgement. So, for exam-ple, the exclusion encountered by disabled children relates to the processes of exclusion concerning childhood and disability. The rights agenda for change in relation to disabled children can be seen within the pressure for inclusive education rather than segregated education from a rights perspective:

> It is about contributing to the realisation of an inclusive society with the demand for a rights approach as a central component of policy-making. This position has been informed by insights and ideas derived from disability studies. This perspect-ive raises some important issues with regard to the question of inclusive educa-tion. First, it encourages the issue of change to be foregrounded. Unlike integration, the change process is not about assimilation but transformation of those deep structural barriers to change including the social base of dominant definitions of 'success', 'failure' and 'ability' within the academy, as well as schools.
>
> (Barton, 2003, 13)

One of the key developments in the legal arena has been the incorporation of the European Convention on Human Rights into English law in 1998, opera-tional since 2000. The system enables children, for example, to apply to domestic courts if they consider a government or public agency has infringed their rights as specified in the European Convention. If the court finds in their favour, then the government is obliged to rectify the situation through a

Table 3.1 Critiques of the UN Convention on the Rights of the Child (UNCRC) and research questions

Critique of the UNCRC	Questions
The lack of engagement with children's political rights	How can children's political rights be best represented political processes in national and local governance? What position can be adopted regarding children's voting rights, for example? See pages 73–4, for further discussion
The lack of substantial involvement of children and young people themselves in formulating the UNCRC	How can this lack be redressed? How can the unique perspective brought by children and young people as experts in their own lives be introduced to the understanding, reformulation and implementation of rights?
Does not pay adequate attention to discriminatory forces which affect children's rights: for example sexism, able-bodied-ism, racism, homophobia	How do issues such as racial and gender discrimination and patriarchy affect children's rights? For further discussion, see pages 95–6 What is the relationship between cultural and religious belief and children's rights? For further discussion, see pages 147–51
Children's rights in relation to areas such as participation are often interpreted as reflecting Westernized concepts that see individuals as autonomous, emphasizing rights such as individual choice. Other cultural ideas which emphasize social cooperation or the centrality of community are often left out.	How can different cultural concepts be reflected in ways of looking at children's rights? For further discussion, see pages 146–7
Aspects of 'identity' not envisaged by the authors of the text are not acknowledged: the idea is that our identities are not established by birth or parents, but made by children within interactions with society: 'A right to an identity could imply anything from respect for chosen (or not consciously chosen) sexual orientation to respect for all the child's efforts to remake his or her identity' (Olsen, 1992, 217)	How can a child's developing identity, in areas such as sexual orientation, be recognized within a rights framework? For further discussion, see pages 73–4 and 117

Source: Drawn from Badham (2004), Childwatch (2006), Jones (2008), Moss (2002) and Olsen (1992).

'fast-track' procedure to bring about legislation in conformity with the Convention (Human Rights Act, 1998, Section 4 (2), 10, Sch. 2).

At a national, or macro, level the literature points to the importance of legislation in promoting children's rights and social inclusion and to the creation of posts such as the Children's Commissioner for Wales. At local level some have said that the UNCRC's emphasis in Article 12 on children's right to participate has been reflected in the increase in their involvement in decision making within areas of service provision such as education, leisure and health. Others have criticized the lack of real engagement in participation to influence decisions and to have their voices acted on. As identified in Chapters 1 and 2, criticism has identified other ambiguities, tensions and omissions within the UN Convention. This includes its lack of enforceability unless it is incorporated though national law, the lack of promotion of children's participation through political rights and that definitions – such as that of the child's 'best interests' – may be made by adults rather than involving children's own ideas and agency and that it does not pay attention to the ways in which forces such as patriarchy within society and families affects children. These critiques can also be seen to form the agenda for enquiry and research presented in Table 3.1.

What are some of the implications of these tensions?

As introduced in Chapter 1's discussion of a 'divided response' (see pages 22–3) and the idea of a 'rights veneer' (see page 26), some have argued that the actual implementation and action on reflecting the UNCRC has been patchy. Some nations have been more concerned with a tokenistic engagement, rather than a real engagement true to the spirit of the Convention itself and actually creating meaningful change for children. The real effects or implications of a rights perspective have been considered in a number of ways. Authors and researchers consider this from different perspectives. Franklin, for example, notes a common theme, that 'the ambitions of the UN Convention have not been fully realized or translated into commonplace entitlements for children in the United Kingdom despite the government's ratification of the Convention a decade ago' (2002, 2). However, he notes improvements, including policy initiatives such as the National Childcare Strategy, and Quality Protects, with its 'strong recommendation' that local authorities appoint a Children's Rights Officer for looked-after children.

Table 3.2 The qualities of rights

Quality of rights	Detail
All rights are limited	Some areas of children's lives can be protected by rights: for example the three 'Ps' can be protected as legal concepts. Some arenas cannot be legislated for by government – so though the UNCRC states the importance of children living in an atmosphere of love and understanding, the law can protect a child from obvious neglect or abuse, but it cannot enforce love
Some rights are aspirational	There are factors that may affect a nation's capacity to realize rights. Hence a lack of resources may have a negative impact on a country's ability to respond to an Article. (see pages 164–6, for further discussion)
Children's rights occur in a context and are conditional, not absolute	The implementation of a child's rights occur within a complex network of factors. The UNCRC states that the rights of the child should be a 'primary consideration' – but they are not the only considera- tion. The relationship between an individual child's situation, the concept and practice of what is in his or her 'best interest', the rights of other people and the role of what is possible within the laws or policies of a country all interact. This can make the idea of an absolute position on implementing an area of rights for every child in the same way can be inappropriate because individual situations must be taken into account in finding a way to engage with his or her rights
Children's rights are shared	Alderson says that the UNCRC is not about 'selfish individualism' but about the goal of equality in social justice and the improvement of standards of life for everyone in a society (see pages 77–8, for further discussion)
Rights are about necessities	They concern areas such as clean water, safety, play (see pages 140–1, for further discussion)
Rights go with obligations and respon- sibilities	Not all children, for example, the very young, can understand and demand rights for themselves. Hence, adults have a responsibility, and the rights in areas such as provision and protection involve duties held by others towards children's access to their rights (see pages 96–7, for further discussion)

Source: Based on Alderson, 2008, 18–19.

Alderson (2008) identifies the following qualities of children's rights developed from the UNCRC as shown in Table 3.2.

When reviewing the way rights are being responded to, it is useful to see them within this framework: as interconnected and as a part of other ways in which children experience their lives within a society. The material from Alderson can help to see how rights, obligations and responsibilities are connected, for example, or to perceive the interwoven relationship between children's rights and the experiences of everyone within a society or community. The framework can also help to understand that, as the previous chapter introduced, rights occur within a context and within a complex of different interests. Olsen (1992) has pointed out that the tensions existing within the UNCRC are illustrative of 'the broader problems of trying to improve the life situation of a group by conferring rights . . . laws conferring rights will have gaps, conflicts and ambiguities' (1992, 213). One example she selects concerns primary education, which is compulsory. Article 28 says that it shall be 'directed to the preparation of the child for responsible life in a free society' (UNCRC, 1989), and the spirit of this is of understanding, peace, tolerance, equality of the sexes and friendship among all peoples. Olsen notes that to those who do not support these ideas 'this direction is likely to sound more like propaganda than education' (1992, 213). Olsen points out that there is a contradiction within the UNCRC itself here – on the one hand advocating the right to a certain kind of education, while, on the other hand, advocating a right to religious views which are in direct contradiction with the values its vision of education promotes: 'this education towards tolerance, equality between the sexes, and friendship conflicts with various religions, which the Convention guarantees to children the right to participate in' (1992, 214).

Tensions and debates: the UK opt-out of the UNCRC – an examination of a 'divided response'

One of the key criticisms of the UNCRC as a force in children's lives is that it need not be acted on in full. This forms the basis of criticism of the UNCRC in terms of its limited ability to enforce compliance with human rights legislation. Comments such as that made in the medical journal, *The Lancet*, are echoed by many agencies and individuals: 'realistically many governments do not take their responsibilities seriously and others are slow to implement change' (Reading et al., 2008, 24).

An example of this 'divided response', as introduced in Chapter 1 (pages 22–3), is the United Kingdom's relationship to the UNCRC. Criticism of the United Kingdom are persistent and vocal, from a number of agencies within the United Kingdom, and from the United Nations itself, yet the government has not altered its position in some critical areas for many years. In 2002, for example, the United Nations Committee on the Rights of the Child's concluding observations on the United Kingdom criticized the performance of the UK government in relation to

- children in the penal system,
- children and 'irregular migrants',
- inequalities in education and health.

Criticism of the UK government's lack of commitment to addressing its divided response to children's rights has come from many different organizations. The Children's Rights Alliance (2008a, 2008b, 2008c), a non-government organization, made a report leading up to the following, 2008, phase of the United Nations cycle of reviewing progress in the United Kingdom. This concluded that the UK government had not significantly addressed the UN Committee's criticisms in relation to children's rights and the treatment of children seeking refugee or asylum, for example. The Report of the 2008 UN Committee echoed this and, again, criticized the UK government for a lack of progress. These issues can also be seen in the UK Commissioner's report (2008) on the UK government's response to children's rights summarized in Table 3.3.

As detailed above, for many years the UK government has *deliberately* retained an opt-out of the UNCRC. This opt out allows child migrants and asylum seekers to be locked up without judicial scrutiny. So, whereas the UNCRC obliges nations to place the 'best interests' of a child first, the opt-out meant that the UK government does not need to apply it to these children. Therefore, officials could lock them up, sometimes for weeks or months pending deportation. The UK Border Agency officially said that they were 'determined to treat children within our immigration system with fairness and compassion' (news.bbc.co.uk/1/hi/uk). However, despite this rhetoric, following an inspection in 2008, HM Inspectorate of Prisons, for example, said that children were detained for too long and were left distressed and scared at the Yarl's Wood Centre in Bedfordshire. The following statement from their 'Report on an announced inspection of Yarl's Wood Immigration Removal Centre' (2008) gives some sense of the UK government's attitude

Table 3.3 Review of 2008 UK progress and children's rights

Issue identified by the Commissioner's Report 2008	Details
The lack of a common understanding of what we mean by children's rights	Children's lack of knowledge of rights as defined by the UNCRC: • deterioration in child mental health • children feel increasingly pressurized, in particular, by school, exams and commercial marketing • protection from domestic violence, parental substance misuse and parental mental health problems These three issues illustrate the lack of awareness and understanding of the impact on children of policy decisions at national and local level
The tension between protection and participation rights influenced by the view of children within society	Overprotective attitude towards children that reduces their opportunities for play, leisure, recreation and healthy development • children feeling unsafe • the treatment of children in the Justice system These three issues illustrate the contradictory perspectives of children as victims and as villains
Whether everyone has equal access to rights	Children seeking asylum • persisting inequality in income, health and education • children in care and leaving care Disabled children's experiences are worse than those of mainstream children

Source: Table drawn from UN Commissioners Report (2008) and CRAE (2008).

towards the best interests and rights of children, when its own inspectorate reported:

> The plight of detained children remained of great concern. . . . An immigration removal centre can never be a suitable place for children and we were dismayed to find cases of disabled children being detained and some children spending large amounts of time incarcerated.
>
> (2008, 5)

Some children and families were being transported to and from centres in caged vans. The report adds,

> prolonged detention was having a detrimental effect on the welfare and behaviour of children whose fear and distress was strongly reflected in our children's interviews.
>
> (2008, 5)

Interviews with the children, some aged between 10 and 11, were made as part of the inspection. The report includes the following:

- One child mentioned that she and her sister were gated apart from their mother and brother in the van. They had only one stop on the way from Dungavel IRC and her sister had had to go to the toilet in the van.
- Three stated that they wanted to go home and were missing family and friends.
- Two were unhappy with the food.
- Two were unhappy as they had been given flight dates that had then been cancelled. One of them stated that staff had given them a flight time at 2/3am.
- One, commenting on the staff, stated 'they're evil' and that there were only two good members of staff.
- One was unhappy because they were ill.
- One was worried when thinking about going back to their country of origin and said 'I feel like I'm in prison, as if I've killed somebody.'
- One was frustrated that they needed their mother to be able to do anything, i.e. dining hall and if they needed the toilet during visits.

(2008, 86)

The report also included parents' perspectives on the children's experiences. Parents were spoken to before interviews were conducted with their children, to explain the purpose of the interview and to request permission to interview their child. No parent refused. Parents raised some concerns about the effect detention was having on their children, in particular:

- One had been doing well at school outside, but had now become very withdrawn. Unlike his brother, he could remember what their country was like and was worried about returning.
- One child had been suffering from panic attacks since arriving at the centre.
- One child had become very withdrawn since entering the centre. They had lost interest in activities, were eating little and slept little as they were awake crying.
- Another child had also had problems sleeping as they were up crying at night and were missing their outside life.
- One child had begun bed wetting and their behaviour had deteriorated, with the child being rude to staff and having to be made to attend school.

(2008, 86)

At the same time as the Commissioner's Report (see Table 3.3, page 70), a campaign was launched by the UK publication, *New Statesman*, around this issue. Its remit was to call on the UK government to end the detention of children for immigration reasons. The presence of the campaign and the response from the UK government's own Children's Commissioner for England are included as an illustration of tensions regarding the role and nature of the UNCRC. The *New Statesman* describes 'No Place for Children' in this way:

> Every year, around 2000 children pass through the UK's immigration detention centres. They are there because their parents have applied for asylum in the UK. Detention is physically and emotionally damaging for children . . . many subsequently receive refugee status, but children who have been detained remain deeply traumatised by their experiences.
>
> (O'Keefe, 2008 www.newstatesman.com/uk-politics)

This example helps to illustrate the way that a divided response undermines a society's response to child rights and the need for rights to be reviewed and pursued within a society. Here voluntary agencies and the media are pursuing the child rights agenda in relation to a group of children who the UK government sees as not deserving the same rights as other children.

Activity 1

Review the material from the HM Inspector of Prisons and their interviews with parents and children (pages 69–71). Professor Aynsley-Green, the Children's Commissioner for England described the way UK immigration system treated children as 'positively cruel' and 'inhuman' calling on the government to 'live up to its rhetoric by making sure every child does matter' (O'Keefe, 2008, www.newstatesman.com.uk-politics).

How do you see this material in terms of children's rights and the UK government's commitment to the following outcomes from Every Child Matters?

- being healthy
- staying safe
- enjoying and achieving
- making a positive contribution
- achieving economic well-being.

(DfES, 2004)

Consider each outcome in relation to the responses to the situation of the children in the Yarl's Wood Immigration Removal Centre as described in the reports and commentaries contained in this chapter.

Activity 2

How do you see your analysis of the situation these children are experiencing in relation to the points made in Table 3.3 concerning 'whether everyone has equal access to rights'?

What is research showing us about tensions and debates concerning children's rights?

The following presents a more in-depth review of the existing literature and research to illustrate the way tensions relating to three key areas relating to the UNCRC and children's rights. The first regards participation; the second, provision and consent; and the third, protection.

Tensions and debates: research and participation

In terms of the right to participation, research has shown that children and young people have varied experiences of developments to date within countries such as the United Kingdom. The following example of research examines an aspect of their experience.

Example of research: children, participation and a rights veneer

Stafford, Laybourne and Hill (2003) interviewed 200 children aged between 3 and 18 years, from different ethnic backgrounds and different social contexts. They were asked what they wanted to be consulted on, and to detail any advice they wanted to give to government and policy makers about consulting children. Comments showed an awareness of issues referred to earlier – such as consultation being a veneer of involvement, without any real impact on children's lived situation:

- If they're not going to do something, don't ask.
- People consulting should not assume young people are going to like adult ideas and give the responses adults want, but ask for young people's own ideas.
- If the Parliament was asking it would be 'Do you think this would be a good thing?,' so that's not actually us deciding things – they're putting it into our heads. . . . We should be asked what our idea is.

(2003, 365)

The children consulted advocated a reduction in the voting age, young people's referenda over 10 on issues such as the presence of attention to lesbian and gay sexuality within education, and young people's representation in parliament (2003, 370–1).

One of the research's conclusions was that young people's experience of consultation had often been 'unsatisfactory' due to two main factors:

- It had not been representative, and
- It lacked impact.

The research revealed that children and young people had a strong wish to be involved and to be consulted, especially on issues directly affecting their lives: education, school, recreation, public transport and health. The children wanted to see results from the consultation and that their participation had an effect: their views being taken into account in planning policies and in decision making. Feedback on the process and results were also seen as crucial. A strong emphasis was placed on recognizing that children's agendas in participating may be different from those of adults: 'allowing children to talk about what matters to them and not dismissing as trivial, children's priority concerns' (2003, 372).

Reflections on the research

Activity 1
How do you see the comments that the young people wanted their 'views being taken into account in planning policies and in decision making' in terms of rights issues, and the notion of a 'rights veneer' as described in Chapter 1 (page 26)?

Activity 2

- Sinclair has said the challenge is to move beyond one-off or isolated consultations to a position where children's rights to participation are 'firmly embedded within organisational cultures and structures for decision making' (2004, 116).
- Care is needed to ensure genuinely open communication in participation rather than seeking confirmation of what adults think or want (Stafford et al., 2003, 372).

How do you see these comments on rights in relation to the interview findings summarised in this box?

This example illustrates how the emergence of a 'rights veneer' needs to be challenged by monitoring to ensure that participation is not qualified by those with power, adults, to result only in changes they feel are confluent within their own agenda. This research helps to illustrate the importance of participation being embedded within processes that result in actual impact and of children being included not only in consultation but also in decision making and in dialogue about the results of their participation.

Tensions and debates: rights, provision and consent – rights-informed ways of relating to children

Lansdowne (1996) points out that the phrases used in the legislation, such as 'best interest and welfare', are invariably defined by adults. Lowden's (2002) work can be seen as an illustrative example of this issue regarding provision and children's rights. She has argued that despite recommendations, guidelines and legislation, the response to ways of relating to children in the light of children's rights, particularly in relation to consent in the provision of health care, remain complex and inconsistent. She points out that though both the Children Act (Department of Health, 1989) and the United Nations Convention on the Rights of the Child (1989) stress the importance of listening to children and taking their views seriously, doctors and nurses are uncertain whether, in relating to children, they should respect children's wishes or whether they risk breaking the law by doing so. She notes:

> Case law in the UK focuses on the end point of decision making, that is consent, instead of the process of sharing information through the stages of investigation, diagnosis and considering treatment options. This amounts to an all or nothing approach, which confers full legal status on competent people but does not attend to participation when patients are partly involved and can influence rather than make decisions.
>
> (Lowden, 2002, 107)

She draws attention to the following issues:

- Children's *experience* can determine their understanding more than *age*, and children with chronic conditions who have repeated treatment have understanding that does not consist of abstract thought but of illness, disability and treatment experience (Alderson and Montgomery 1996a, 1996b).
- From this experience young children understand the value of life and can weigh up alternatives and express consistent values based on a firm sense of identity, thus demonstrating the moral and rationale basis of wise decision making. Therefore, to test competence in the *abstract* without reference to the *circumstances* may be misleading (O'Neill, 1984).
- Laws that allow treatment to be forced on non-competent children appear to assume that they have no understanding worth considering. However, very young children do reason and can perceive unexplained treatment as assault and as far more damaging than the disease it is intended to treat (Alderson and Montgomery, 1996a, 1996b). This opens a credibility gap between the child's perception of harm and the adult's intention of benefit.

She argues that the greatest obstacles to children being asked for consent arise from adult prejudices about their abilities and the protectionist view of the rights they can, or do, have. Lowden concludes:

> At present childhood belongs to children least of all and its study remains largely a study of adults' attitudes to and practices with children. Children are not human becomings they are human beings at birth and they have particular views about their own status. Children are people in their own right and as such should be recognized as having rights. (Qvortrup et al., 1994)
>
> Lowden (2002, 107)

She reflects that in the United Kingdom the 'historical evolution of childhood' continues to influence children's rights. This means that rights do not exist in a vacuum and that factors such as cultural attitudes towards children affect the ways relationships are formed or the ways policies are created and responded to. Lowden argues that adult beliefs about children's rights influence children's opportunities for self-determination. Her argument is that until adults develop a more pragmatic ideology regarding children's rights, a true respect for children's autonomy will not be achieved and that areas such as consent will remain an adult and legal prerogative.

Activity 1

From this discussion how do you see the relationship between rights, consent and the ways children–adult relationships are formed? Again, based on this discussion of Lowden's commentary, how can her critique help see how positive changes can be made in relation to children's experience of consent giving?

Activity 2

In relation to the above material, Lowden (2002) comments,

> Children will not be facilitated to develop competence and thus the process of 'best interests' will continue to be defined from a protectionist adult perspective.

How do you see this relating to the comment in Table 3.2, that 'The UNCRC states that the rights of the child should be a "primary consideration" ' – but that they are not the only consideration? Discuss this in terms of the relationship between an individual child's situation; the concept and practice of what is in their 'best interest'; the rights of other people, such as parents or carers; and the role of what is possible within the laws or policies of a country.

Tensions and debates: Rights and child protection – a rights agenda

Reading et al. (2008) show how a rights perspective can alter the way an arena of children's lives is responded to, by forming a rights agenda for change as introduced in Chapter 1 (pages 16–18). Their work also questions some of the divisions often made between areas which can be considered as a 'rights'-related issue and those which are often separated off as not concerning children's rights. They review the way child 'maltreatment' is looked at. They argue that the most prevalent way of looking at it is as a public health problem, or concerning harm to individuals, but less often as a violation of children's' rights. They argue that the UNCRC provides a framework for

> understanding child maltreatment as part of a range of violence, harm, and exploitation of children at the individual, institutional, and societal levels. Rights of participation and provision are as important as rights of protection. The principles embodied in the UNCRC are concordant with those of medical ethics. The greatest strength of an approach based on the UNCRC is that it provides a legal instrument for implementing policy, accountability, and social justice, all of which enhance public health responses.
>
> (2008, 3)

They argue that further incorporation of the UNCRC principles into research, laws, policy and training of professional will result in 'progress' in the area of child protection. They also link child maltreatment to a rights based perspective on poverty arguing that in

> child maltreatment the risks associated with poverty and inequalities, socially vulnerable families and the intergenerational cycle of deprivation and violence are well recognised. Strategies for prevention of maltreatment are recommended to target these high-risk groups, and intervention programmes are advised to be sensitive to social inequalities and not to inadvertently widen them. However, poverty can be represented as a violation of children's rights. The universal declaration of human rights grants the freedom from want; article 27 of the UNCRC recognises the right to a 'standard of living adequate to the child's physical, mental, spiritual, moral and social development' and the concept of rights as capabilities for living (e.g. the capability to be alive, healthy and have self-respect) justify the argument that poverty infringes on children's rights by prevention of their optimum development.
>
> (2008, 3)

They cite an approach that avoids blaming individuals, and, though, it does not 'absolve them of responsibility', it sees the state as accountable for improving social justice as a 'direct intervention to prevent maltreatment' (2008, 20). Hence, they argue such a 'rights based perspective allows risk factors to be reformulated as instances of discrimination, exclusion and victimisation', with social isolation and unemployment seen as 'violation of children's rights of protection, provision, or participation either explicitly as mandated under the articles of the UNCRC or less directly' (2008, 20). Following on from this they argue that reinforcement of laws affecting discrimination and social divisions are a powerful way of approaching child maltreatment.

The following example looks at another angle concerning rights and protection, showing how research is enabling insight into the nature of children's rights, the responses in areas such as policy making and the implication for children's lives.

Example of review: rights, protection and privacy – tensions, spaces and relationships

Analysis by Dowty (2008) identifies how information technology (IT) is being used to monitor children's lives. Her review included the following range:

- The use of CCTV in schools and nurseries,
- Smart card technology that allows monitoring of children's meal choices, library borrowing and registration,
- Mobile phone software that allows parents to track their children,
- The growing use of national databases that collect and increasing range of data on all children,

Dowty suggests that this combination can

> produce a situation where a child cannot eat chips, visit the toilet or deviate from a pre-ordained route without somebody else knowing about it. Every test result, absence or means of travel to school is captured. Personal profiling tools, behaviour records and practitioners' observations of whether a child's friendships are appropriate, their aspirations realistic or their spare time put to constructive use create a rich seam of data that can apparently be mined for signs of trouble, or to make actuarial assessments of potential problems in the future. It is now possible for children to be under intense scrutiny by one means or another, and the speed, capacity and interoperability of information systems ensure that the assembled data can rapidly be conveyed to others.

Reflections on the review

Activity

The rationale behind these initiatives concerns the 'protection' of children.

What do you think the dangers are of this degree of, or approach to, protection?

How do you see it relating to the ways in which children can be protected while maintaining an appropriate degree of autonomy and privacy?

What tensions can you identify in terms of thinking about who should be involved in deciding what an appropriate degree of autonomy and privacy is?

This material illustrates the importance of a rights agenda being connected to other forces at work within society: it shows how emergent thinking argues that it is vital that the rights agenda be understood within a wider framework. It also demonstrates the complexity within the implementation of a rights-informed approach to relating to children and that our understanding of how to respond effectively to areas such as protection is still evolving: how research and analysis is helping develop insights into the nature of children's rights and responses in areas such as policy making and its implications for children's lives.

Activities

The following activities are designed to help reflect back on some of the key concerns over the chapter as a whole.

Chapter activity 1

The CRAE report in Chapter 1 quoted a child saying that

> *They think because we're small and they're big*
> *they know better . . . and they just treat us like we're*
> *nothing, like we're just a puff of cloud or something.*
>
> (Child under 11)

In this chapter Lowden's comments on consent are referred to

> Case law in the UK focuses on the end point of decision making, that is consent, instead of the process of sharing information through the stages of investigation, diagnosis and considering treatment options. This amounts to an all or nothing approach, which confers full legal status on competent people but does not attend to participation when patients are partly involved and can influence rather than make decisions.

Consider these two quotations. How do you see them in terms of the following?

- The possibilities of developing a rights informed way of redefining relationships between adults and children, and
- Children giving consent in a health context as a child rights issue.

Chapter activity 2

Look back through the different examples of research within this chapter, and the analysis of the material. Examine the ways in which you think they offer useful ways of thinking about children's rights and set agendas for new directions in thinking about children's rights. It might be helpful to use some of the ideas in Chapter 1 to help structure your thoughts. Consider the ways in which the material helps develop or rethink ideas and practices of children's rights in terms of the following:

(a) A rights dynamic: 'the ways in which a rights dynamic has been created . . . [this] . . . concerns the ways in which the ideas about rights have been applied in order to affect . . . laws or policies.

(see page 13)

(b) Rights-informed ways of relating to children: 'enabling children to be seen and to be treated differently by adults. It is part of shifts in the ways in which children and young people see themselves, their relationships with each others, individual adults, groups they encounter and braider organisations that they connect with in their lives such as local or national government.

(see page 19)

Summary

The following summarizes some of the key issues identified within the review of the development of ideas and practices, enquiry and research in this chapter:

This chapter has

- reviewed the ways tensions, ambiguities and gaps within legislation have been identified;
- explored the ways these phenomena reflect issues concerning the relationships between international, national and local application of rights-based approaches to children's lives;
- examined tensions and debates concerning research and participation;
- examined tensions and debates concerning research, rights and consent;
- examined tensions and debates concerning rights and protection.

Further reading

Broadhead, P., Meleady, C. and Delgado, M. A. (2008) 'Valuing children means valuing families', in *Children, Families and Communities*. Maidenhead: Open University Press, 25–35.

A clear example of consulting children about service provision in Sheffield's Children Centre from a rights perspective.

Jones, P. (2009) 'How are otherness and childhood connected?' in *Rethinking Childhood: Attitudes in Contemporary Childhood*. London: Continuum.

Considers the ways in which negative stereotypes of children have developed and how this affects their position in society. It explores the development of new ways of seeing children from a rights perspective and how these are affecting children's lives and those who live and work with them.

Research details

Example of research: children, participation and a rights veneer

Stafford, Laybourne and Hill interviewed 200 children aged between 3 and 18 years as a response to the 'recent surge of interest' in consulting children and young people about issues affecting them. This article is based on what children have said about consultation.

Stafford, A., Laybourne, A. and Hill, M. (2003) ' "Having a say": Children and young people talk about Consultation', *Children & Society*, 17, 361–73.

Example of review: rights, protection and privacy – tensions, spaces and relationships

Dowty responds to policy and practice that uses IT, identifying, recording and tracking children in England under the banners of child protection, reducing risk and improving outcomes. It argues that there is a need to review such developments in the light of a child's right to privacy. It also considers whether placing faith in unproven technology may inadvertently increase levels of risk to children.

Dowty, T. (2008) 'Pixie-dust and privacy: What's happening to children's rights in England?' *Children & Society*, 22, 393–9.

Part 3
Implications for Children's Lives

Rights and the 'Child's Voice'

Chapter Outline

Introduction and key questions   85
What is the meaning of 'child's voice'?   86
How does 'voice' relate to rights?   90
What is research revealing about rights-informed practices relating
to voice and participation?   95
Summary   108
Further reading   108
Research details   108

Introduction and key questions

The idea that adults should make decisions for children and should speak on their behalf has been part of the ways many children experience their lives and the spaces they live in, whether at school or attending hospital, from the design of their playgrounds to the way they are treated in law courts. Recent theory, research and practice have started to rethink and challenge the assumption that adults should automatically represent children in this way. Research has been used to assert the right of children to participate in particular ways, to have a voice that is heard and engaged with. This chapter examines the development of the idea of rights and the 'child's voice' along with the implications for children and for those living and working with them.

> What is the meaning of 'child's voice'?
> How does 'voice' relate to rights?
> What is research revealing about voice, participation and rights?

What is the meaning of 'child's voice'?

The term 'child's voice' is a metaphor. It has come to represent a cluster of ideas and issues. In many instances when 'voice' is referred to in relation to children, it is used to address its opposite: children's experience of being silenced, when adults have not listened to children, or have put words in their mouths.

This silencing is not voluntary on the part of the child. It is something which is either actively done by others, or which occurs through the ways in which factors in society result in children being silenced and excluded. This chapter will look at how recent challenges to these processes have developed from the dynamic created by the ideas and practices of children's rights. It will look at how research is contributing to a changing climate for children and adults concerning rights and participation. A key concept will be that of a rights-informed way of relating to children in terms of participation.

On the one hand, recent years have seen a developing agenda within many countries that children should be able to express their opinions, be involved in decisions and be aware of the factors that influence any decisions that affect them. So, for example, in the United Kingdom, the Human Rights Act, 1998 (Article 10), requires the government to uphold the right to freedom of expression, while the Children Act (1989) requires local authorities both to ascertain the wishes and feelings of children they look after and to give these 'due consideration'. Table 4.1 (page 87) illustrates how this agenda is expressed through research furthering these right-driven goals.

Structures and procedures developing from such research include the following:

- Frameworks and principles for obtaining children and young people's involvement within the work done by government departments,
- Children's and young people's councils,
- Requirements for service providers to involve children and young people in the way they work.

Initiatives include children's representation on school councils, consultative processes involving government policy development and implementation and practices such as youth advocacy.

On the other hand, research has constantly pointed out the complexity of this aspect of child rights. It has helped identify the advances and limitations

Table 4.1 Voice and research: rights-driven goals

Area	Issue	Source
Law	Children's views being adequately represented in courts – participation, protection and provision rights	James, A. and McNamee, S. (2004) 'Can children's voices be heard in family proceedings? Family Law and the construction of childhood in England and Wales', *Representing Children*, 16(3), 168–78
Democratic involvement	Case study research into young people's involvement in rural and urban local government in Australia – participation and provision rights	Sligo, J. (2003). *Young People's Participation in Local Government Initiatives: Rural and Urban Case Studies* (Research Summary Report). New Zealand: Children's Issues Centre, University of Otago
Awareness of their own rights	Children's perceptions of the UNCRC and its impact on their lives – participation, protection and provision rights	Sandbaek, M. and Hafdis Einarsson, J. (2008) *Children and Young People Report to the UN on Their Rights* (Annex to Norway's Fourth Report on the Convention on the Rights of the Child). Norsk institutt for forskning om oppvekst, velferd og aldring NOVA – Norwegian Social Research

of attempts to elicit and involve children's voices. In addition, research is revealing that although providing laws, guidance on practice and processes for children's participation are important, other connected matters must be engaged with. If the complex interrelationship of factors silencing children are not addressed, research has shown that they will hinder or halt attempts to enable children to have voice, to participate.

The complex factors silencing children can helpfully be seen in three particular ways:

- The worth of children's voices,
- The ways that social exclusion silences children,
- The dominance of adult orientated ways of communicating and decision-making.

The first centres on children's voices not being given *worth*, in terms of adults not treating their ideas or opinions as having value or legitimacy. Here the idea of 'voice' is attached to areas such as judgement, maturity, capability and power.

adults not valuing childrens opinions

turn over →

Adults are in positions of power in areas such as decision making and responsibility, and children are excluded from holding and using power. Their exclusion can be termed as having no 'voice' or power in making decisions. This absence of voice and power is seen within large-scale decisions in government through to children's everyday lives at school or at home.

The second concerns the ways in which a variety of factors to do with *social exclusion* interconnect in the silencing of children. These concern how people are excluded within society, and these are additional forces which add to the ways in which children are not given voice. Such factors include the ways in which poverty, class, gender, race, sexuality or disability affect children's lives. Rivers and Cowie's (2006) research, for example, illustrates how the silencing of children can be combined with other factors which exclude and silence children who are lesbian or gay:

> a high percentage of victimized students remain silent about their distress. The percentage of pupils who tell their teacher or anyone at home that they have been bullied increases fairly consistently with frequency of being bullied, especially for the highest reported frequency of 'several times a week'; but even for these, only about a half of secondary pupils tell anyone at home. Some victims may seek help from peers, teachers, or parents. However, many withdraw, staying silent about their suffering. Since the admission of being upset can provoke derision or hostility from peers and retaliation from the bullies, it often seems safer for a victimized young person to silently endure the abuse.
>
> (2006, 12)

The third is the assumption that *adult modes of communicating* are the only way that participation can be valid. This is embedded in many aspects of most societies: communication, consultation and decision making are made through the adult-orientated written word or speech. Here 'voice' is seen as something that is *articulate* only in particular ways and that articulacy is given to a certain status: the position of the adult. Children who do not communicate like 'mature', 'articulate' adults are not seen as having a worthwhile contribution to make. This assumption is reflected in many formal and informal structures and ways of working: the way organizations function, the kinds of language used, the way relationships are formed and the time devoted to an action or process. So, for example, decisions might be made based on information provided in a way that is only accessible to adult ways of communicating, interactions between people are handled in a way that children do not understand, or the longer time needed to assimilate or decide on something is not provided for.

Children are taught to assume that they do not have voice, in the
they are encouraged to believe that adult's voices serve them in m;
their lives.

If we think about the metaphor of the child's voice it's possible to say that,
taken literally, having a voice means being able to speak or express yourself out
loud. Looked at in this way it is about the act of being able to articulate in certain ways, to communicate. It is also about having something to say: experiences, opinions, ideas. It is about being heard or listened to by others and your
words having an impact. It is about your words having an impact. Table 4.2
draws together the discussion so far to show the different aspects of these ideas
of 'voice'. The picture from theory, research and practice can be seen as

Table 4.2 Silence and voice

Child's silence	Child's voice
Children's lives and experiences not worth attention In areas such as the law or education, the main focus is on adult or parental interests Main focus in areas such as legislation, the law is on adult or parental interests with children being seen as dependent, as the property of parents and as being of lower status and value	Children's voice is to do with children's lives being worthy of attention and being given value
Children not seen to be able to articulate anything about themselves of any worth Adults represent children and their 'best interests': only adult opinions about children and adult ways of valuing what happens to children are valued	Children able to represent themselves and to have opinions and input that matters Children have a perspective that is different from that of adults, and that this is of equal value to that of adults
Children's role is to listen to and be looked after by adults. They are best served by adult actions based on adult experiences and judgements of children's needs or adult intentions for children's development and future Services such as education, health or social care are structured and delivered in ways that are devised and implemented purely by adults	Children are active and able participants, capable of judgement and insight. They have opinions and input of value, and are experts in their own lives They should have input into the services that work with them
Children are immature and what they think and say cannot be trusted Adults create relationships and organizational structures that assume and assure that children see their own ideas and expressions as of less value and status than that of adult	Children are capable and are able to have input in ways that encourage and develop their capacity as decision makers and valid contributors

revealing tensions to do with children's voices being silenced, devalued, or ignored, compared to their voices being articulated, heard and responded to.

On a macro level, the issue of children's voice is seen in terms of children representing their interests, experiences and particular perceptions in areas such as the development of policy. This includes acknowledging their status as citizens with rights to be involved. Some research has investigated the way children can participate in decision making about national agendas. Other work has focused more upon their engagement with areas of their lives that affect them in relation to the micro level of immediate service provision in their daily lives. This has ranged from policy making about education and health, through to the management of particular organizations such as schools or day care services that they are served by, or in the day-to-day running and experiences of a provider such as a health centre.

How does 'voice' relate to rights?

Contemporary ideas about the child's voice often refer to the UNCRC's Article 12 and its assertions about participation. As discussed in Chapters 1 and 2, this states that children and young people have a right to a say on all issues that affect them, and for these views to be taken seriously (UNCRC, Article 12). One of the key issues here is that children are seen to have a *right* to be involved: 'children's participation is a value or rights based principle' (Franklin and Sloper, 2005). This engages voice and participation within a framework of rights and responsibilities. In addition, this is seen to be connected to the idea and practice of seeing children as citizens with rights in the present, rather than as future citizens with full membership being granted upon their reaching adulthood.

The following Key Points show some of the key issues connecting voice and participation rights:

Key points: voice and participation rights

- Representation – creating processes and spaces that allow children to represent themselves, or to have their position represented without adult bias;
- Impact – the idea of that a child's voice -their opinions, choices or ideas – should have an impact by being engaged with, responded to and acted on;

⇨

- <u>Judgment</u> – to view children as capable of judgement and encouraging processes that inform children, give them information and support them to make judgements about issues that affect them;
- <u>Validity</u> – the idea that a child's voice has validity and meaning, that their perceptions are as valid as, or, in certain contexts, more valid than, adults' opinions and ideas.

Within these areas of representation, impact, judgement and validity, the notion is that children are often excluded from processes that connect with their lives. The exclusion from arenas such as informing government decision making, family decisions, is held to be due to attitudes and existing structures that are specifically prejudiced against children. These reflect and re-enforce the stereotypes outlined in Chapters 1 and 2, that treat children as incapable, innocent or not competent.

On a micro level research has looked at how that the concept of the child's voice alters the way adults see and hear children and the ways adults see and hear children in their everyday interactions with them. This has been seen in terms of the different sites, role and relationships or types of interactions, as shown in Table 4.3.

Research has begun to re-examine these sites, role relationships and interactions using a framework of rights-informed ways of relating to children.

Table 4.3 Sites, roles and relationships

Site	Role (child–adult)	Traditional type of relationship or interaction (child–adult)
School	Pupil–teacher	Passive–active Consumer–provider
Hospital	Patient–doctor	Needy/ill–expert Powerless–powerful
Home	Daughter/son–parent	Cared for–carer Protected–protector Weak–strong Decision follower–decision maker Rule follower–rule maker

Example of research: school and voice

Kilkelly et al.'s (2005) research with children revealed that having a say in decisions made about them was the most important rights issue identified by them. Nearly a substantial amount of the children's comments related to school (90%), and many of these concerned not having a voice in decisions within school life. Typical comments included the following:

> Sometimes school can get on my nerves cause I don't think children get enough respect from teachers and caretakers and I think some children are scarred [sic] about speaking their mind in case they get shouted at.
>
> (Girl, aged 11 years; Kilkelly et al., 2005, 186).

The following presents some of the conclusions from the research with illustrative quotations:

Research conclusion	Sample of children's comment from research
Pupils acknowledged power and status were problematic in having their views acknowledged	'Pupils don't really have a say in school. Teacher's opinions always come first' (Girl, aged 14; Kilkelly et al., 2005,186).
Children's views were not listened to	'Some teachers get on to you without listening to what you are saying' (Young person in focus group; Kilkelly et al., 2005, 181)
Participation was often perceived as tokenistic with a gap between views expressed and any action or feedback	'As soon as you got in it was just like you got handed the minutes from the last meeting and you had to talk about this and this and it was mainly about the canteen and stuff and you didn't really get the opportunity to bring anything up' (Kilkelly et al., 2005, 187)

Reflections on the research

Activity

The research's findings, on a small scale, reflect the much larger-scale recent criticisms made by the United Nations Committee on the Rights of the Child regarding the UK government's relationship to rights and children's participation. In its reports the Committee has criticized the United Kingdom for issues relating to its lack of compliance to the Convention. The following areas related to the gap between rhetoric and actual practice in terms of voice and decision making in education and parallel the quotes from the children in Kilkelly et al.'s (2002, 5) research findings:

The committee commented on:

a. the failure to solicit school children's views in relation to issues such as sex education and school exclusions.

(2002, 3)

b. the lack of action 'in education, school children are not systematically consulted in matters that affect them'.

(2002, 7)

c. the government's need to 'take further steps to promote, facilitate and monitor systematic, meaningful and effective participation of all groups of children in society, including in school, for example, through school councils'.

(2002, 7)

Reflect on your perceptions of the relationship between Kilkelly's research and the areas noted in a, b and c.

Recent scholarship, research and policy is focusing upon rights and the child's voice in relation to *increasing* children's participation and involvement. On a national governmental level this is to do with the ways in which children are consulted and listened to in relation to existing, or future, policies. In relation to national and local service provision a similar focus is placed upon children being consulted about provision and development in areas such as health care or play. Attention has also been given to children's voices within their family or immediate support networks: the extent of their involvement in areas such as decisions relating to divorce or within therapy dealing with family difficulties. An example from the UK's Department of Health makes a clear distinction between *consultation alone* and *participation* that results in empirical *impact* through actions that occur as responses to children's views or expressed opinions:

Participation should go beyond consultation and ensure that children and young people initiate action and make decisions in partnership with adults, for example, making decisions about their care and treatment or in day to day decisions about their lives.

(Department of Health, 2002, 4)

Researchers such as Lewis (2009) offer a critique of the idea and practice of the 'child's voice', examining the ethics and purposes behind such engagement with children. Her work advocates a reflective approach to understanding the motivations behind accessing children's 'voice'. Her approach describes five methodological aspects of such work: recognizing, noting, responding to, interpreting and reporting from children. As with other researchers in this area, a part of her critique concerns the importance of being wary of the appearance of consultation, providing a veneer, without any real engagement with the content of the material accessed through such practice. There are three main themes that researchers and commentators have highlighted within such criticism and the rethinking of the 'child's voice'. These are between children's *consultation*, *participation* and the key issue of *impact*.

Key points: consultation, participation and impact

Approaches and methods

One theme concerns the search for approaches and methods that can be used by adults and children to communicate in ways that enable children to participate effectively. An example of this might be how to enable children to be given information and how to empower them in understanding information and responding to it, communicating their ideas and thoughts. This is an example of a rethinking of children's participation informed by a rights agenda.

Acting on them

Another theme focuses upon whether children's ideas, suggestions and decisions are actually acted on or allowed to have any impact or whether adults and adult organizations pay lip service to the idea of participation, while only acting on the children's input that fits what adults wanted to hear or what they wanted to do. An example of this might be a school that asks for children's views in a school council, but then is either highly selective about what children are asked about, or ignores their input when it contrasts with what adults want to do. This can be seen as an illustration of challenging the response to the idea of children's rights that creates a 'rights veneer', rather than a full engagement that acts and responds to children's rights to provision or participation.

Challenge/impact

The third area tends to challenge the idea of involvement and participation in relation to the dominance of adult-created structures and ways of operating. This challenge argues that children's points of view and position in society offers a radical challenge to adult approaches: proposing that children should be at the heart of setting up and devising all child services. This approach argues that setting up a new school, for example, should involve children from the very outset in the devising of the building, employing staff and setting up the school's structures. This can be seen as an illustration of rethinking how adults and children work together: a rights-informed way of relating to children and their spaces.

As mentioned at the start of this chapter, research has explored how other structural inequalities re-enforce or add to the ways children are excluded and silenced. Factors such as gender, poverty and race add to the ways in which children are excluded, and are seen as rights-related issues.

The Irish Refugee Council statement from 2006 shows how these are related in relation to asylum seeker children, for example,

> Separated children – children outside their country of origin separated from parents or other caregivers – are invisible in Irish society. This invisibility is two-fold, first as children who often have no voice and secondly as asylum seekers, marginalised in society. If these children are largely invisible in the first instance, who will notice if they go missing? Who will advocate on their behalf and play surrogate parent to remind the State that its obligations under the UN Convention on the Rights of the Child apply to all children within its territory, be they citizens or not.

(www.irishrefugeecouncil.ie/press06/separated_children.html [accessed 12 June 2008])

When looked at in this way, the barriers to participation experienced by all children become added to by other forces of social exclusion concerning, in this example, racism and attitudes towards asylum seekers. This illustrates how factors involving voice, exclusion and discrimination are complex and multiple and how important it is, when trying to understand and respond to the silencing of children to look at the different factors which combine to affect them. The next section explores these issues further.

What is research revealing about rights-informed practices relating to voice and participation?

The following looks at the three key areas identified earlier in the chapter, illustrating different ways in which research is exploring and developing our response to rights and children's voices:

- The worth of children's voices,
- The ways that social exclusion silences children,
- The dominance of adult-orientated ways of communicating and decision making.

The worth of children's voices

The tendency has been to link the worth and validity of a child's voice to adult opinions about appropriate 'levels' of competency and capability. This has often involved drawing broad lines about competency based on factors such as age. Current developments in thinking, research and practice are questioning this. The following illustrates research that questions assumptions about age and a child's right to have their voice heard.

Example of research: child's voice and age

Flewitt (2005) looked at how 3-year-old children use a range of 'voices' during their first year in pre-school. The study worked with the children at playgroup and at their homes. The research identified the following:

- The children make sense of their world through means other than speech.
- They express themselves 'multimodally' through combinations of talk, body language, facial expression and gaze.

The conclusion was that there were distinct patterns and that children used different communicative strategies. These related to the dynamics of the institutional and immediate contexts in which they were situated.

The findings implied that the current focus on talking in early years provision may be detracting from children's capability to communicate and be involved in their world, as it does not reflect the diversity of the ways children make and express meaning.

Within this research the idea of the child's voice relates to representation in that it argues that the children in the study, due to their age, are representing themselves not through verbal speech but through other means. Hence, the adult conception of how an individual represents him or herself and his or her wishes, needs or wants, are challenged by the child's broader and different ways of communicating. In addition this approach starts from a view that looks for capability and as much involvement as possible, rather than looking at deficits in verbal communication and comprehension.

Hence the impact of children's voice is reduced until adults alter their way of approaching 'valid' communication and look to maximize a child's involvement. From this, it follows that these children can have more impact on what happens to them by the difference of their voices being acknowledged.

This challenges the power relations of communication and opinion where adults deem small children to have no capacity or capability. Traditional adult views of how old a child can be before they are seen to have *any* capacity to judge or communicate their judgements are shown to be based on questionable preconceptions about age and voice. The research shows that looking at child-based ways of encountering communication can allow these aspects of a child's voice to be seen and acted upon differently.

This research asks at what age should children have a right to be heard? In addition, it challenges ideas that there can be a notion that a child 'comes of age' at a certain point, or to be deemed 'capable' of being heard, and advocates the position that there are differing degrees of being heard and different kinds of competency.

Reflections on the research

Activity 1

This research originates in ideas that value engaging with children in ways that are rooted in children's capacities to communicate and to be involved rather than adult ideas about what is valued. How do you see the following in relation to the research contained in this box?

- The worth of children's voices,
- The ways that social exclusion silences children,
- The dominance of adult orientated ways of communicating and decision making.

Activity 2

Franklin and Sloper have discussed the UNCRC's Articles 12 and 13, rights and worth in the following way:

> While it is arguable that Article 12 is limited by reference to particular attributes of the child, namely their capacity, age and maturity, Article 13 grants children the right to express, seek and receive information in any medium they wish. This emphasis on provision of appropriate means of communication is of particular significance to younger children and disabled children, especially those with communication related impairments.
>
> (2005, 21)

The following is a quote from the UK's Department of Health statement regarding this issue, that, for example, a child who is learning disabled should not be assumed to lack competence: 'many children will be competent if information is presented in an appropriate way and they are supported through the decision-making process' (Department of Health, 2001, 4).

They draw these together to conclude that

> Parents and health practitioners have a clear duty under Article 12 to ensure that the child has been given both the time and information they need to be helped to make an informed choice.
>
> (2005, 21)

How do you see Franklin and Sloper's points concerning children with disabilities in relation to the conclusions of the research contained in this box?

The ways that social exclusion silences children

Research has revealed that, while in a number of countries legislation and practice has begun to reflect children's right to express their views and to have them acted upon, broad factors that exclude sectors of the population have an impact on children's participation. A review of research by the Joseph Rowntree Foundation concluded that the indications were that

> many professionals fail to consult with or involve disabled children, even where statutory duties require authorities to ascertain children's wishes and feelings, as in The Children Act 1989, The Children (Northern Ireland) Order 1995, and The Children (Scotland) Act 1995. In addition, disabled children and young people are often excluded from wider consultations around local policy and planning, their neighbourhoods and communities.
>
> (www.jrf.org.uk/knowledge/findings/socialcare/741.asp)

Rights and inclusive education for disabled children are intimately connected. UNESCO, for example, frames the 'human right to education' as the core of inclusive education in its working document 'Inclusive Education: Public Policies' (UNESCO, 2008). Its review of research and practice summarizes this view as concerning the ways in which 'a rights-based approach establishes the rules against all grounds for discrimination in education such as gender, disability, caste, ethnicity religion, race, economic status, refugee status and language' (2008, 3). Tomasevski (2004) described this agenda as being founded upon three principles:

- Access to free and compulsory education;
- Equality, inclusion and nondiscrimination;
- The right to quality education supported by concrete conditions, inputs, processes and outcomes.

The 2008 UK Children's Commissioners' Report to UN Committee on the Rights of the Child summarized the situation in the following way, highlighting the relationship between voice, exclusion, decision making and the need for training, alongside attitudinal and structural change:

> Disabled children and young people are much less likely than those without disabilities to participate at any level, particularly those with complex needs or with only non-verbal communication. Research has shown only a small number of disabled children are involved in decisions about their care. Many professionals lack

understanding, hold assumptions and/or underestimate disabled children's competence and ability to participate (Franklin and Sloper, 2007) Other research found that it is common for professionals to record that a child's level of impairment prohibited their wishes from being ascertained (Stuart and Baines, 2004). Despite new statutory duties on public authorities to promote positive attitudes towards disabled persons and to encourage participation by disabled persons in public life, there is limited evidence of the impact of these duties on the lives of disabled people. Moreover, the duties have yet to be implemented by a number of authorities.

(2008, 19)

The following is an example of research that examined ways of challenging the exclusion experienced by disabled young people by exploring effective ways of creating access to participation, decision making and impact.

Example of research: 'Ask Us!'

'Ask Us!' involved work in several different sites in the United Kingdom. The project involves disabled children and young people, led by The Children's Society with joint funding from the Joseph Rowntree Foundation. It developed from the UK's Department of Health's National Disability Reference Group for a programme called 'Quality Protects'. Its objectives include improved involvement and services for disabled young people and their families (Badham, 2004). Some of the key aspects of the work are described as

- being centred on active involvement and consultation with disabled children and young people and
- including children with a wide range of abilities and disabilities including some with severe and multiple impairments. Some, for example, were described as not using 'speech or sign language; they express their wishes and feelings in other ways.'

The project examined the ways in which multimedia methods could be used to make the consultation more inclusive. Hence children and young people were supported in choosing their own means of communication. The consultation happened over three months in order to allow time adequate to explore and develop the variety of communication processes used, and to enable relationships to develop . Children and young people identified five basic questions:

What do you enjoy?
What do you want more of?
What are your experiences of consultation?
What are your experiences of participation and of services?
What do you understand by inclusion?

An example of the use of multimedia to establish and communicate concerns involved the use of images, such as graphics and cartoons to express issues; video; and songs devised by the children and young people and distributed on CD ROMS on areas looking at exclusion in play, education and leisure, for example. Badham notes that the work was rooted in ideas expressed at the beginning of the of the CDROMS made to record and communicate the work:

> with disabled young people declaring that participation is manip- ulative if it does not lead to improved services. 'Know Your Rights!' calls out one young man (Ask Us! 2003). They go on to show the practical changes needed to fulfil their rights.
>
> (Badham, 2004, 148)

The project involved ascertaining the practical impact of the research into what the children and young people wanted changed, and the impact of the initiative on those involved and the people and organizations involved. The conclusions from the young people included the following:

- Changes in adult attitudes that enabled them to see young people as active agents and as capable experts in their own lives;
- Reframing the consultation processes of organizations to include appro- priate engagement of young people, using methods that recognized the different capabilities of the young people and that had adequate resourc- ing to permit the methods to be used, adequate time to conduct the research at a pace appropriate for the young people and disseminating the findings in ways that were accessible to the young people;
- New training to enable new methods to be developed and used;
- Change in priorities that focused on the involvement and ideas of the young people.

A summary described issues emerging as including:

> Some disabled children relied on communication aids and/or people who know how they communicate. But these aids and people were not always available in all parts of their life (e.g. leisure time as well as at school) or when they moved or left school. Young people felt this denied them their right to speak.
>
> (www.jrf.org.uk/knowledge/findings/socialcare/741.asp)

Specific projects looked at particular issues that concerned local children and young people. The following is a summary of some of the work in Solihull:

> St. Christopher's Solihull: three young people led their own research on the usefulness of helplines in local authority complaints leaflets. They got some training on basic research methods, and led the research at all stages. In the same project, four disabled children and five of their non-disabled

friends did an access audit on eight local parks over one weekend. They called it "Can we go to the park, mom?" and used videos, digital cameras and pictures to record the results. The audit highlighted the inequalities experienced by disabled children in accessing everyday opportunities and local facilities.

(www.jrf.org.uk/knowledge/findings/socialcare/741.asp)

In analysing the effectiveness of this work the following factors were identified:

- It is important to give each project resources to use flexibly and creatively.
- Young people were often involved in all stages of the consultation.
- Giving appropriate tools and support to all children, including those who were labelled as having 'severe or profound disabilities' and 'challenging behaviour'.
- Using the multimedia approach enabled the children and young people to communicate their views to a wider number of people, nationally and in the areas they live.

Young disabled people who were paid as researchers described feeling valued and responsible; they enjoyed the work and felt they benefited from meeting other disabled people and hearing their stories.

(www.jrf.org.uk/knowledge/findings/socialcare/741.asp)

Reflections on the research

Activity 1

How do you see each of the following in relation to the research contained in this box?

- The worth of children's voices,
- The ways that social exclusion silences children,
- The dominance of adult-orientated ways of communicating and decision making.

Activity 2

In reviewing this research Badham has concluded:

This is a long way from participation as empty consultation rhetoric. Participation becomes the means of achieving change on issues raised by young people, with adults joining in rather than taking over, and Government implementing specific changes as a result, through improved play resources locally and, through national policy development, promoting accessible play provision across the country.

(Badham, 2004, 150)

Review this description of research by Badham and consider the relationship between his comments and the work of 'Ask Us!', particularly concerning the following:

- Participation and change,
- Adults joining in rather than taking over,
- Local and national change.

Interview with Maureen Murray about the 'Ask Us!' research

Maureen Murray, 'Ask Us!' Children's Society

Phil Jones: How do you see the value of 'Ask Us!' In terms of the involvement and participation which the research comments on?

Maureen Murray: 'Ask Us!' educates people on the importance of including disabled children/young people in processes. It acknowledges they have a valuable contribution to make and evidences that they know what they want to say, particularly disabled children/young people with profound communication difficulties, who are rarely asked, but often have the most to say!

The Children's Society's belief reinforces this: that the determination and imagination of disabled children/young people who want to be understood should be matched by those who they need to understand them.

The DVDs are a powerful tool that are 'timeless' – they can be shown and used in a variety of forums with messages directly from disabled children/young people themselves. Delivered in a way that they 'say it'.

The 'Ask Us!' methodology enabled disabled young people to use whichever means they wanted to get their message across [photos, video, songs, questionnaires, drawings etc.]. It ensures the involvement and participation of disabled children and young people is on the young people's terms, is meaningful to them and fun.

Phil Jones: How do you see 'Ask Us!' in terms of children and young people's rights?

Maureen Murray: Disabled children and young people have a right to be listened to, valued and have a say in all things that affect them and their lives as set out in the UN Convention on the Rights of the Child and the UN Convention on the Rights of persons with Disabilities as well as a range of UK legislation, regulation and guidance. 'Ask Us!' gives disabled children and young people an opportunity to express their views and opinions. It challenges negative perceptions and systems that can be a barrier, which prevents them taking part in mainstream life, as other children do. It is an empowering and enabling tool. This is what disabled children/ young people themselves told us:

- We want to go where other children go
- We want to do what other children do
- We want to be listened to
- We want to be respected
- We want to be consulted
- We want to feel the same buzz as other people do
- We want to have a say in things that affect us
- We want to be A PART of our community not APART from it!

Phil Jones: How do you see the value of children and young people in 'Ask Us!' being involved in carrying out their own research?

Maureen Murray: Disabled children/young people are the experts!!!! They must be valued for who they are and be seen as contributory members of society and not passive recipients of care and services.

It is important to support disabled children/young people in all of our research programmes allowing them to challenge themselves, each other, systems and other professionals, in a partnership of mutual trust and respect.

'Ask Us!' continues to provide new learning opportunities for both disabled children/young people and those who find out about our work. Existing skills can be refined and developed, and new skills acquired. This can be done in a safe environment where mistakes can be made, risks can be taken and lessons can be learnt.

It fosters inclusion, equalises opportunities and allows disabled young people to take control, be less dependent, develop a positive self-image and become more assertive.

Disabled young people, like other young people, may choose to get involved at different levels. 'Ask Us!' enabled some young people to be 'researchers'. In relation to 'Ask Us!', and in 'Ask Us 2!', 49 disabled young people were trained, supported and paid as young researchers. They took part in planning the work, selecting the broad topic areas, carrying out consultations, filming activities, narrating, editing, and in the latter stages dissemination at conferences and workshops. Many more young people were consulted and actively shared their views contributing material for the CD ROMs.

Most importantly disabled young people were in charge of the medium and the message. They researched issues and helped create the multi media means of recording them. They were supported in choosing their own means of communication, not straight jacketed by standardised forms and professional norms.

The value can be judged in terms of the empowerment of the young people who have been involved but in the end the young people themselves have to judge the value of their involvement. We know that for some young people they will judge the value on whether or not they were instrumental in achieving change – not necessarily just for themselves but in relation to the lives of many more other disabled children and young people. As one young person said,

'if one person sits up and realises that disabled children and young people have a voice then it was worth doing.'

(Quote taken from The Children's Society's Vision, Mission and Values)

The dominance of adult-orientated ways of communicating and decision making

MacNaughton et al. (2007) examined ways of challenging aspects of the barriers to children's right to participate, looking at approaches to challenging adult-orientated ways of communication and involvement in participation. Their work focused on young children, and is rooted in the relationship between rights and voice:

Adults' views are valued according to their proponents' social identities (e.g. their class, 'race' and gender); and on the rare occasions when children's views appear in public debates, they are rarely regarded as equally valuable as adults' views. Thus, listening to young children is the first step to regarding children's rights as rights of citizenship, rather than as rights defined – and restricted – by age.

(MacNaughton et al., 2007, 466)

They say that adults face two major tasks in relation to this listening and 'including younger children's voices' (2007, 466):

- to enable young children to express their opinions confidently, and
- ensure that those opinions are taken seriously.

Example of research: consultation with young children

MacNaughton, Smith and Lawrence (2003) initiated a consultation exercise with young children from birth to eight years. They used an action-learning model to assist 23 early childhood staff to consult children about their experiences of their education and care services.

This drew on a combination of methods designed to enable a child to work with the language or process the child wanted to and could express themselves through. These included pictures, photographs as well as words. Most children were in the age group of 3 to 5 years, with 8 of the 173 children aged less than 2 years.

The researchers worked with key questions:

> What do children think they need for their well being?
> What do children wish for and value in their lives?

The children's views covered three arenas of their life: their experiences of family and home, of education and of care. In relation to their family and home, for example, the children's priority was to have a safe and caring family with whom to spend time, and most children felt safe with key people in their families. Many children also wanted a home in which members of the family have time together and time apart. The findings included the following:

> Girl – 'I feel special when I'm with my family';
> Boy – 'I feel safe when I live in a house so the rain and thunder don't get you';
> Girl – 'My family is special because they are always there for me';
> Girl – 'Home is a place where I can be myself'.
> Girl – 'I'm happy in this picture at the lucky, lucky preschool because it's not noisy there. There aren't too many kids. The teachers sit down and talk to you all the time. They let you decide what to do all the time. They don't tell you what to do'.

The authors argue that this kind of approach reinforces the growing body of research evidence that young children

- are quite capable of expressing their views on things that affect them and that they value;
- enjoy the opportunity to do so;
- can be worked with in ways that encourage and assist them to develop the knowledge, skills and confidence they need to become active citizens who can participate actively in public decision-making.

(2003, 465)

They conclude that honouring children's rights to express themselves and their lives creates more effective policy; it results in a more inclusive community and moves towards healthy democracy. However, they note issues concerning power and voice are both crucial to engage with and form a key challenge to young children's voices being heard and empowered (2003, 466).

Research in Norway with slightly older children offers insight from children and young people on what they thought was effective within school systems on their views being engaged with through the schools council system.

⇨

The qualitative interviews revealed that staff-pupil relationships were considered by the children to be crucial to the success of participation. The pupils cited a number of examples of good groundwork by teachers:

> At lower secondary schools the pupils' council had a greater say; the teacher who assisted them was very good. She listened to what we had to say and took the matter up with the school board. We exerted a lot of influence compared with pupils at upper secondary school.

> At lower secondary school the teacher left the classroom for maybe half an hour, so we could discuss in class any problems we had concerning the teacher, or with anything else. It wasn't always easy to talk about these things with the teacher present.

> (Sandbaek and Hafdis Einarsson, 2008, 24)

Reflections on the research

Activity 1
Summarize the key points about important issues regarding children's voices being engaged with from the UK research with young people and the research with the Norwegian pupils.

Activity 2
How do you see the quotation from the UK Research, 'honouring children's rights to express themselves and their lives create more effective policy' (2007, 466), in relation to the points made by the Norwegian pupils?

Activities
The following activities are designed to help reflect back on some of the key concerns over the chapter as a whole.

Chapter activity 1
One of the individuals who worked within one of the service areas examined by the children and young people involved in 'Ask Us!' summarized the benefits from his perspective, particularly the importance of the following:

- Sustained contact
- Build up of trust and recognition
- Recognition of mutual benefit
- Time to move from general issues to specific actions and plans
- Being allowed the freedom to access the work
- Don't be afraid of the message back

- Continue the dialogue; be clear about what can and can't be done and what we can do together
- Implement the changes and let people know what you have done.

(Badham, 2004, 16)

Reflect on the relevance of this worker's perspective to the examples discussed in this chapter.

Chapter activity 2

Dalrymple's review of advocacy services draws on research into young people's experience of the provision. A number of the findings were positive, speaking of how with an advocate 'you're treated like an adult' and shifting from a position in case reviews where 'not having an advocate in the review I didn't get in what I wanted to say. It gives you confidence' (Dalrymple, 2005, 7). Others, however, saw the process of being supported to have their voices heard in a different way:

> Personally I don't feel I can influence things. Even now everyone has closed ranks. But at the last meeting having an advocate in the room meant I felt I could (influence things) and I wasn't taking the whole lot on my own.
>
> (Dalrymple, 2005, 8)

> I wouldn't say its useful 'cos it ain't – it makes it uncomfortable for kids 'cos staff want to know what's going on. They're all sweety sweet for when Inspectors or the psychiatrist comes to the house but then they change.
>
> (Dalrymple, 2005, 9)

Each of these examples, in part, shows how adult attitudes can sabotage attempts to enable children and young people to have their say. Consider any of the research examples in this chapter and

(a) reflect on how adult attitudes might sabotage the work to enable children's voices to be represented,
(b) review what processes could help reduce or stop this occurring,
(c) in the light of your reflections and review, examine the importance of the points made by the National Youth Agency in their guidance on 'Avoiding the traps' regarding children's rights, voice and participation:

- involve children and young people in the earliest stages of planning;
- start slowly, proceed carefully and draw on pilot projects;
- take time and ensure there are the relevant resources;
- recognize and enable the wider changes in attitudes, behaviour and power required; and
- provide consistent support and staff development for steady progress to spread.

(The National Youth Agency, 2005)

Summary

This chapter has

- looked at the meaning of 'child's voice',
- examined how ideas of 'voice' relates to child rights,
- explored how ways of relating to children and young people can silence and disempower and harm them,
- examined ways in which a child rights agenda challenges ideas and practices that silence them,
- reviewed research in order to look at ideas and approached that effectively involve children and young people.

Further reading

Kellett, M. (2010) 'The Research Process Reviewed from a Children's Rights Perspective' and 'Children and Young People as Researchers', in *Rethinking Children and Research*, London: Continuum.

An examination of child research from a rights' perspective, not only featuring illustrative studies about the exercising of those human rights but also discussing what rights children have in the research process itself, and a review of approaches involving children undertaking and leading their own research. Within this paradigm, children set their own research agendas, explore issues about their lives which they, rather than adults, determine are important and research them from their perspectives.

Lewis, A. (2010) 'Silence in the Context of "Child Voice" ', *Children & Society*, 24(1), 14–23.

Offers a critique of the idea and practice of the 'child's voice', examining the ethics and purposes behind such engagement with children. The article includes recommendations for researchers working in the fields of 'child voice' concerning five methodological aspects: recognizing, noting, responding to, interpreting and reporting silence from children.

Madge, N. (2006) 'Collecting the Evidence', in *Children These Days*. Bristol: Policy Press.

A detailed description of two surveys in primary and secondary schools, gathering views and opinions. A detailed description of the process of consultation, the gathering and analysis of data.

Research details

Example of research: school and voice

Research involving children and young people's perceptions and opinions involving focus group work, available at www.niccy.org, including a children's and a young person's version.

Kilkelly, U., Kilpatrick, R., Lundy, L. Moore, L., Scraton, P. Davey, C., Dwyer, C. and McAlister, A. (2005) *Children's Rights in Northern Ireland*. Belfast: NICCY and Queens' University of Belfast.

Example of research: child's voice and age

Flewitt looked at how 3-year-old children use a range of 'voices' during their first year in pre-school, investigating how they make and express meaning 'multimodally' through combinations of talk, body movement, facial expression and gaze in the two different settings of home and playgroup. This was a longitudinal ethnographic video case studies of four children, two boys and two girls.

Flewitt, R. (2005) 'Is Every Child's Voice Heard? Researching the Different Ways 3-year-old Children Communicate and Make Meaning at Home and in a Preschool Playgroup', *Early Years: An International Journal of Research and Development*, 25(3), 207–22.

Example of research: 'Ask Us!'

'Ask Us!' involved work in several different sites in the United Kingdom. The project involved disabled children and young people and was led by The Children's Society with joint funding from the Joseph Rowntree Foundation. It was developed by the United Kingdom's Department of Health's National Disability Reference Group for a programme called 'Quality Protects'. Its objectives include improved involvement and services for disabled young people and their families.

Badham, B. (2004) 'Participation – for a Change: Disabled Young People Lead the Way', *Children & Society*, 18, 143–54.

Details of the Children's Society and 'Ask Us!' Can be found at www.childrenssociety.org.uk

Example of research: consultation with young children

MacNaughton, Smith and Lawrence initiated a consultation exercise with young children from birth to 8 years of age in the United Kingdom. They used an action-learning model to assist 23 early childhood staff to consult children about their experiences of their education and care services.

MacNaughton, G., Smith, K. and Lawrence, H. (2003). *ACT Children's Strategy – Consulting with Children Birth to Eight Years of Age. Hearing Young Children's Voices*. London: Children's Services Branch, ACT Department of Education, Youth and Family Services.

5 Rights and Decision Making

Chapter Outline

Introduction and key questions	110
In what ways does decision making feature in children's lives?	111
What is the relationship between children's rights and decision making?	114
What tensions are emerging concerning decision making and children?	116
What does research reveal about the impact of new thinking and practice in relation to rights and decision making in different spaces within children's lives?	125
Summary	132
Further reading	132
Research details	133

Introduction and key questions

Decision making occurs in children's lives within a wide range of spaces: from domestic decisions about what to do or where to be in their home or community, to educational decisions about the way a school is regulated through a school council, for example. It relates to all areas of children's rights: to liberty and welfare rights, to participation, protection and to provision. Those adults involved in decision making vary in terms of their roles and relationships with a child: these include family members, professionals such as teachers, doctors, the police and those involved in local, regional, national and international government. Children's rights have recently been at the fore of questions which are being asked about the very varied treatment and experience of children in relation to decision making in their lives. However, across all of these different arenas and varied contexts or types of interactions, recent developments and research have concerned certain emergent themes or tensions regarding children and decision making. The following questions will be used in this chapter to draw out these tensions and themes, rethinking decision making from a rights-based perspective:

> In what ways does decision making feature in children's lives?
> What is the relationship between children's rights and decision making?
> What tensions exist in contemporary society about decision making in children's lives?
> What does research reveal about the impact of new thinking and practice in relation to decision making in different spaces within children's lives?

In what ways does decision making feature in children's lives?

Decision making relating to children happens in ways that involves direct personal interaction with a child: for example between a father and a small child in the home, or in a playground, or between a teacher and a child in a large classroom group. Decision making relating to children can also happen in ways that do not often involve face-to-face interactions: for example, in committees involving the creation of policies, or within government involving law making. The literature also reveals the ways in which different disciplines see children and decision making, and how these ways have an impact on whether and how children are involved in decisions that affect them. These include conceptual frameworks from developmental perspectives which relate to how ideas about 'maturity', age and cognition are seen, for example, and which are reflected in children's encounters with the law or medicine. From political and sociological perspectives emerge issues about the ways in which negative traditions and stereotypes upheld by adults about children's capability and capacity affect the way areas such as the law or health services view and treat children's decision making.

The following offers some brief illustrations of the wide range of issues and contexts within which children's decision making is currently being reviewed in practice and research. The Australian National Childcare Accreditation Council, for example, gives a flavour of approaches that are developing that lay emphasis on children as *decision makers* at a very early age:

> Children can be involved in decisions about:
>
> - whether to play alone or in a group, be involved in a quiet activity or to be physically active
> - which materials and experiences they will engage with; the opportunity to choose those things that interest them and match their level of competence
> - what happens to them in relation to their physical care. For example, nappy changing, toileting, sleeping and eating
> - whether they want to do things independently or would like some help
>
> (www.ncac.gov.au/factsheets/factsheet2. Page 1)

Other perspectives on children and decision making examine it within a personal or family sphere, and link it to psychological and emotional development in areas such as self-esteem. The following, for example, is from a US-based perspective on working with children aged between 4 and 8 years:

> - Decisions about personal issues: 'Do you want to color with crayons or colored pencils? Would you like to wear your pink blouse or your blue blouse?'
> - Decisions about family issues: Family rules e.g., time for bed, length of phone calls, morning routines, homework and family work responsibilities, and any other activities which help your family run smoothly.
> - When decisions meet the needs of other people, children see themselves as having a meaningful impact on other people. In this way, decision making continues to enhance self-esteem.
>
> (Willis, 1998, 3)

Another important perspective sees decision making in terms of structural political frameworks. In a different arena of decision making, and in relation to older age groups, Combe's (2002) discussion of a survey of local government in the United Kingdom, for example, notes that initiatives such as 'Quality Protects' and 'Connexions' specifically require the *involvement* of young people and link involvement to decision making. Combe concludes that the survey revealed that many councils are committed to 'including young people in decision-making' around policy priorities such as the Community Strategy, the Neighbourhood Renewal Strategy and the New Deal for Communities programme. She goes on to assert that from the six focus groups run by the research with young people across different age groups,

> Young people may feel disconnected from political debate and decision-making but they are interested in a wide range of political issues.
>
> (2002, 5)

This LGA/Institute for Public Policy Research survey was responded to by 55% of the authorities in England and Wales: of these, over three-quarters had established youth forums and councils. More than nine out of ten of the responding councils cited gaining information on young people's views and improving service delivery as the most important reasons for involving young people in decision making. The City and County of Swansea is cited by Combe as demonstrating 'flexibility to young people's needs in their initial steps to involve young people' (2002, 7). The council initiated a series of focus groups involving over 350 young people to find out issues of concern. Issues raised in the consultation were expanded on at a youth conference. Combe notes that the relationship between consultation, on the one hand, and real impact on actual decisions made, on the other, was not unproblematic:

> However, less than one in three local authorities responding to the survey evaluated the impact of initiatives involving young people in decisions.
>
> (2002, 7)

Issues concerning the different levels of the engagement of children and young people in decision making are also revealed as an issue within research. Franklin and Sloper's (2006) survey of social service departments in England, for example, reflected this type of division in their results analysis:

> Encouragingly, disabled children were being involved in different decision-making areas, although it would appear that quite a majority of children's involvement in service development so far has centred on what could be termed 'children's issues' – activities, equipment or décor, which are more concrete concepts and within a child's own experience. Involvement of disabled children and young people at a higher strategic level still seems to be rare.
>
> (2006, 731)

This illustrates the different spheres of children's lives within which decision making occurs and how exclusion can vary between these arenas, with adults permitting access to some areas, but not to others. It also shows how factors such as the social divisions of society and the ways adults relate to children as gatekeepers for access to rights affect the way decision making is experienced by children.

What is the relationship between children's rights and decision making?

The material examined so far has seen decision making from a variety of inter-connecting perspectives: psychological, emotional and social development, for example, or in relation to politics and healthy democracy. This section focuses upon ways of viewing children's decision making from a *rights* per-spective. The US organization 'Youth on Board', for example, sees decision making *primarily* as a rights issue. They frame it in a way that makes clear the relationship between rights, decision making and childhood:

> Nowhere in the U. S. Declaration of Independence is there a stipulation concern-ing age. 'All men are created equal,' all are entitled to 'certain unalienable rights'. So why is it that in this country, decisions that affect a significant segment of the populations are made by others? In far too many situations, young people are not being heard. Their rights are being disregarded or violated, and adults do not seem to hear or care about it. This needs to change. A shift is needed in our com-munities to allow young people's concerns to be heard and taken seriously. They have the same right as adults to voice their hopes, ideas, and fears.
> (Youth On Board, 14 Points: Successfully Involving Youth In Decision making, Youth on Board • 58 Day Street • Somerville, MA 02144 • 617.623.9900 x1242 www.youthonboard.org page 1)

Decision making, when looked at in this way, can be seen to relate to liberty and welfare rights and a child's right to participate as defined in the UNCRC. As referred to earlier, traditional practice in many societies, and in many cultures, has largely involved adults making decisions about areas of chil-dren's lives and the spaces they live in – such as education, health or leisure. Key transitions and events in a child's life can occur without any attempt to involve a child in them. Tomlinson describes the situation in the following way:

> The complexity of ideas about childhood and the ways these are drawn on by poli-ticians is often overlooked. Where children are concerned they may be viewed solely as economic investments. Their care and welfare might be considered but their status in society as full human beings far less so . . . where the child is the centre of consideration, the emphasis has tended to be on their welfare and the role of the family rather than their status in society.
> (2008, 29)

She contrasts this position with one that views children as citizens 'as holders of human rights too' (Tomlinson, 2008, 29) and argues that this can be allied with the need to acknowledge 'the power of children and their participation in political and economic decision making' (Tomlinson, 2008, 29). The picture which has emerged from research into children's experiences of spaces such as home, school, hospital and the streets of the communities they live in is one in which it is routine for adults to behave in ways that assume that the following is quite normal for adults:

- to make the decisions about what children can do, and how they live within the spaces they inhabit
- to regulate children's and lives through formal laws, and the way they treat children more informally through rules and attitude, as if children either do not have the capacity, or right, to be involved in decisions about the way they conduct their lives.

Examples of this are included in the following key points.

Key points: spaces and norms in decision making

Space	Issue	Norms in decision-making processes
Education: school	Which type of education provision a child receives: which school to attend	Parents decide on options offered by adult education workers with no requirement for children to be involved
Education: school	School exclusions	Teachers and parents or guardians decide with no requirement to involve or hear a child within the decisions made and actions taken
Law: courts	Sentencing in Youth Courts	Decision are made by adults with little or no involvement of the child in the analysis and discussion of the situation
Health: medical centres and hospitals	Which treatment options are to be taken	Doctors and parent/guardians make decisions with no requirement to involve children in decision making or to act on decisions made by the child themselves

⇨

Activity 1

Consider the decisions listed in the column titled 'Norms in decision making processes':

i. Reflect on your *own* experiences of decision making in each area – either your experiences as a child, or an adult. In particular, consider whether you as a child, or you now as an adult, experienced each of these in a way that is reflected by the 'norm' described, or whether your experience has been different? For example, in the norms concerning education – has your experience been that adults decide, or were children involved in the decision making about which type of school was attended?

ii. Reflect on different ways in which children could be involved in decisions in each of these arenas. Ask yourself what assumptions you are making about why, how and whether children can be involved in decision making.

Activity 2

Consider the earlier quotation from Youth On Board:

> In far too many situations, young people are not being heard. Their rights are being disregarded or violated, and adults do not seem to hear or care about it.

How do you see the connections between this quote and the material in the table about 'norms' and children's spaces?

The following examples examine children's lives in the light of a rights based approach to decision making and illustrate how this perspective challenges long held assumptions and ways of working.

What tensions are emerging concerning decision making and children?

The struggle, as described in Chapters 1 and 2, between traditionally held views of children that hold them as incapable or innocent and the framework emerging from the new sociology of childhood is reflected in debates about decision making and child rights. This section looks at two key arenas of children's lives as an examples of rethinking rights in terms of this struggle and tension. It draws on children's experiences in the spaces of education and then law to look at the complexity of issues concerning decision making and rights in some detail.

Decision making and participation rights in education: which school?

Children spend much of their time, when awake, in school spaces, or pursuing school-related activities in their home environment. The UK government, for example, has increasingly emphasized the school as the physical location for a number of services for children and as a fulcrum for arenas of a child's life in areas such as health, welfare and play. Hence, the nature of the school space and the processes concerning schooling are key to any child. However, in the United Kingdom this crucial arena of a child's life is largely the domain of adult decision making, with children and their experience of the main space in their lives treated as the recipient of adult decisions. They are disenfranchised from the right to participate in most aspects of decision making within their main space in their life, concerning areas such as the direction and regulation of educational experience and school life. Local authorities are legally obliged to make arrangements for enabling parents to express preferences about the nature and use of this space, but are under no such obligation to consider the wishes of a child 'by, for instance, allowing the child to make submissions as to what type of educational provision would best suit him or her and at which school the child wishes to be educated' (Anderson, 2008, 20). Codes of Practice concerning school admissions often make no mention of the participation of children in decision making concerning schools admissions (DfES School Admissions Code of Practice, DfES/0031/2003).

Anderson (2008), for example, has noted that the Committee on the Rights of the Child maintains that the right to participation contained in Article 12 applies to all other rights contained in the Convention and to 'all measures adopted by States to implement the Convention' (UN Committee on Rights of the Child, General Comments No 5: general measures of implementation of the Convention. On the Rights of the Child parts 4, 42 and 44. CRC/GC/2003/5 (2003) para 12).

Anderson's analysis helps to see the connections between the right to participation and the decision-making process in terms of problematic issues arising within many children's experience of education:

> The Committee has specifically stated that the rights to participation is important in ensuring a child's right to education, and child rights within the education system: 'education must be provided in a way that . . . enables the child to express his or her views freely in accordance with article 12 (1) and to participate in school life' (UN Committee on the Rights of the Child, Gen Comment No 1: The Aims of Education, CRC/GC/2001/1 2001, para 8).'
>
> (2008, 18)

This means that children should be able to participate in decision making in areas such as the type of education provision they receive. So, for example, a child should

- decide on which school they attend,
- whether they should attend a special unit or not.

Children should be involved in:

- the running of the school
- the recruitment of staff
- the formulation of disciplinary policies
- curriculum development
- policies on teaching methods and staff development.

Anderson notes that this should also be interpreted to mean that any child should be 'enjoying the right to appeal school admission and exclusion decisions' (2008, 18):

> According to article 12 of the UNCRC, individual children should be afforded the right to participate in educational decisions affecting them. In addition, at a broader level, children's views should be sought in the development of school and government policies, procedures and rules in relation to education.
>
> (2008, 19)

The treatment of children in terms of their rights to be involved in decision making in education varies between societies. Some have developed a more positive response to this aspect of children's relationship to their experience of education (Cohen, Moss, Petrie and Wallace, 2004). Others, such as the United Kingdom, have been criticized for their lack of progress by comparison, and the lack of structured, embedded engagement with children as decision makers. The UNCRC periodic review of the UK government notes in 2002, for example, that obligations relating to Article 12 were not consistently incorporated in legislation. In terms of education, it criticized the UK government, saying that it needed to take further steps to promote, facilitate and monitor 'systematic, meaningful and effective participation of all groups of children in society, including in schools (para 30)', in a way that 'reflects article 12 and respects children's rights to express their views and have them given due weight in all matters concerning their education' (UNCRC Concluding observations: UK of Great Britain and Northern Ireland (2002) CRC/C/15/Add. 188, para 48).

Anderson comments that, despite this indictment from the UNCRC in 2002, over five years later,

> the government has failed to implement these recommendations and ensure that children in England enjoy the right to participate effectively in the education system.
>
> (2008, 19)

Activity
Decision making and School

- Why do you imagine adults would want to exclude children from decisions about their choice of school?
- How do you think children could be involved in decision making in the following areas:

  a. Children deciding about early years setting of choice?
  b. Children deciding about their secondary education?

The right to appeal school admission decisions is conferred to the parent; children do not have a separate right of appeal.

- Why do you think it might be important for *children* to have a right of appeal?
- Why do you think the law has been structured in a way that stops children being able to appeal?
- What do you think this says about the way adult–child relationships are currently seen by the fields of law and education in terms of children's decision making?

Parallel processes can be seen in the ways children are excluded from decision making in a different space – that of the law courts. The following example considers this from a rights perspective.

Example of research: decision making and participation rights in youth courts

Kilkelly's (2008) research into Youth Courts in Ireland draws parallels and differences between children's experience of decision making in Ireland and that of other countries. Kilkelly's enquiry can help to identify the experiences of children and young people in this area in terms of decision making and the relationship between professional practice, adults and children.

Kilkelly notes that

> it is clear from international standards of children's rights that young peo-
> ple have the right to be tried by a tribunal which takes their age and
> maturity into account, which protects their right to privacy and which
> facilitates their ability to understand and participate in the court process.
> Efforts must be made to adapt the court physically and procedurally in
> order to vindicate the child's rights.
>
> (Kilkelly, 2008, 45)

The research, based in detailed observation of Irish Court proceedings looked at the involvement of young people in the processes surrounding decisions made relating to their lives and their future. The following issues were examined – whether the young people

- were included or excluded in proceedings;
- were consulted or ignored;
- were talked about in the third person, as if not present; and if
- any attention was given to whether they could even understand what was happening to them within the decisions

By examining this research we can see not only how the young people were, or were not, involved in this crucial area of decision making, but also, as argued earlier in this chapter, can see how decision making cannot be isolated as a discrete phenomenon, but is interconnected with other issues and processes.

Kilkelly contextualizes the research's observations within the Children Act 2001, Section 96 which states that: 'children have equal rights to adults and, in addition, that they have the right to be heard and to participate in any proceedings of the court that can affect them' (2001 in Kilkelly, 2008, 53)

The research firstly looks at the environment in relation to young people's participation in the processes at work:

> The courtrooms in Limerick, Cork and Waterford constitute. . . . formal
> and traditional court environments. Each court has a raised bench where
> the judge sits, with a further row of the bench in front to accommodate
> the clerk. Solicitors and the prosecutor sit in front of this and the young
> person tends to sit somewhere in the gallery as there is no specially
> assigned seat. . . . The fact that there is no dedicated place for the young
> person to sit/stand means that they can and do sit anywhere. Most young
> people in the proceedings observed sat or stood near the door, or towards
> the middle or rear of the courtroom. Few chose to sit at the top of the
> court, where their solicitor invariably sat, unless they were directed to do
> so (which in itself was rare). The impact of this physical detachment of the
> young person from the other persons involved in the proceedings was
> observed dramatically reinforcing the isolation of the young person from
> the proceedings; this was particularly so where acoustics were poor . . . the
> failure on the part of the young person's solicitor to ensure they are well

placed in the court at least to hear the proceedings, if not also to ensure they have the opportunity to participate directly in them.

(2008, 52)

How do you think the space and the description of the way the space is used might impact on the young person's involvement in the court?

Interactions and involvement in decision making

Kilkelly then summarizes the way interactions occurred between the young person and those involved in decision making. The following give examples of his key findings:

a. Those who wished to speak for themselves, and to follow what was going on appeared to find participation difficult if not impossible.
b. Some were ordered to be quiet or to let their solicitor speak on their behalf, whilst others' efforts to intervene went unnoticed.
c. In 55 per cent of the cases no communication between judges and young people took place: the judge did not greet young person, did not speak to them at any stage, and did not explain proceedings had been concluded.
d. The young person was frequently referred to as 'he' or 'she'.
e. The young person was observed frequently staring at the floor or ceiling or chatting to family members.
f. Some did not realise their case was over until the next case was called.
g. When interaction did take place between the judge and the young person it was usually minimal in nature involving a basic greeting at the start and the end of proceedings.
h. On rare occasions the interaction between the young person and the judge was aggressive with the young person being ordered about, insulted or reprimanded about his/her dress or posture. In a small number of cases, efforts to engage the young person were made by the judge who addressed him/her by name and wished him/her good luck at the end.
i. The young people were often visibly surprised at being spoken to, but appeared overwhelmingly pleased at being spoken to by name.

(2008, 51–2)

Take three of these many examples of the findings from (a) to (i) and identify how you imagine these impact the young person's experience of decision making.

Language as exclusion from decision making

Kilkelly also presents a section of the research's findings about the way language is used by the judges and solicitors. Here, again, is a representative sample of the findings.

a. There was no adaptation of language: 'normal legal jargon and explanations are used.' Examples of this included electing trial in the circuit court and the imposition of bail conditions: 'with little or no attempt to adapt the explanations to facilitate their understanding by young people of varying ages and capacities'.

(2008, 51)

b. In most cases the young person did not speak, nor was he/she spoken to.
(2008, 46)

c. Kilkelly noted that when asked questions about issues or the final court decisions: 'young people frequently responded to such questions with blank faces or looked to their solicitor of family for assistance.'

(2009, 51)

d. Kilkelly found that: 'on the small number of occasions when young people were asked to explain what their bail conditions meant, for example they were unable to do so. One boy asked what a curfew was simply shrugged his shoulders. Another, when questioned about his breach of an order not to trespass in a particular area answered, 'but I was just walking through.'

(2008, 51)

Reflections on the research

Activity 1

How do you see the relationship between the young people's experience of the decisions made as reflected in points (a) to (d) above with the earlier citation of the Children Act 2001, Section 96:

children have equal rights to adults and, in addition, that they have the right to be heard and to participate in any proceedings of the court that can affect them.

(2001 in Kilkelly, 2008, 53)

Activity 2

Killkelly concludes from the research that

- the Children's Court continues to operate like an adult District Court and inadequate attention has been given to how to transform the court into a specialized forum for dealing with age appropriate manner.
- not sufficient attention is paid to the rights of young offenders; their right to a fair and expeditious hearing in the presence of their parents, and their right to be heard and to understand the proceedings that have such a dramatic affect on the lives.
- inadequate efforts to deal with any individual in terms of their specific maturity, or intellectual and emotional capacities, and young offenders' special difficulties in these areas.

- There needs to be:

  age-appropriate language;
  a clear structure to explain the processes and procedures to young people.
  (2008, 53)

Re-examine three of the points from 'Interactions and involvement in decision making' (page 121) (a) to (i) above and think about how these three points from Kilkelly's conclusions could be used to help change the way the Youth Courts are conducted to assist the young people's engagement with the decision making process.

Activity 3

The following presents findings from reviews and research into youth justice situations in two different countries, New Zealand and the Netherlands:

a. In New Zealand youth courts have a number of differences from adult courts

   First the sentencing process is largely in the hands of the family conference, whose findings the judge is expected to endorse. Second, judges are expected to try and involve young people and their parents in the court processes and decisions, and to avoid the issue of court orders unless absolutely necessary. Thus, while generally speaking, the youth court is run in much the same way as the adult criminal court, except that it is closed to the public, in reality it is a recognizably different forum.
   (Morris, 2004, p. 45)

b. Recent analysis of Dutch court practise shows that 'the proceedings are first and foremost a dialogue between the juvenile judge (magistrate) and the young offender' (Weijers, 2004, 28). The conclusions of the review was that whilst legal jargon and court-specific abbreviations are frequently used,

   the practice of the judge in the Dutch youth court is to ask at various points whether what they are saying is clear to the young offender . . . characterised by a 'moral dialogue' whereby the juvenile court usually undertakes some discussion with the offender about the consequences of his/her wrong-doing and in most cases puts questions to him/her that attempt to stimulate feelings of empathy for the victim and reflect on the impact of the offence
   (Weijers, 2002)

Consider these ways of working in relation to those found in Kilkelly's research and compare them in relation to

- the way the relationships of the professionals involved relate to the young person involved,
- the ways the processes at work concerning decisions are made explicit to the young person and how they enable the young person to engage with them.

Interview with Ursula Kilkelly about her research

Dr Ursula Kilkelly, Faculty of Law, University College Cork, Ireland

Phil Jones: There are many issues raised within your work as described in this section. How do you see the research in relation to children's rights and decision making?

Ursula Kilkelly: My research on the Irish Children Court was fundamentally about children's rights in the youth justice process insofar as it attempted to measure the extent to which children in the Children Court participate in proceedings against them. In this regard, it was an attempt to take existing European Court of Human Rights (ECHR) law, notably the finding of the ECHR in *T v UK* and *V v UK* that children have the right to participate effectively in criminal proceedings against them, and to apply it directly to the practical context of youth court proceedings. In this way, I wanted to observe the extent to which children are currently involved in proceedings against them with a view to assessing compliance with ECHR and international obligations.

I chose court observation as the means by which I would do this. So, the research did not directly address the issue of children's decision making, other than to attempt to understand the extent to which children are involved in those decisions that others in the criminal process make about them. This threw up all sorts of issues including, for example, the appropriateness of the adversarial criminal process to respond to offending by young people. The observation also made it clear, almost instantly, that the physical environment of the courtroom was the single biggest barrier to the child's participation in the process. The absence of a place to sit or stand meant that no one prioritized placing the child at the centre of the process; this frequently allowed the lawyer and the judge to have a conversation about the child, almost as if he/she were not there.

Phil Jones: What did you discover, or learn, about the process of research?

Ursula Kilkelly: The research was relatively novel, at the time at least, in that it attempted to develop a set of factors from ECHR and CRC standards to apply to law in action. This was, and remains, an inexact science but in essence I wanted to see to what extent children were involved in the proceedings against them. I decided, because of my limited resources and skills, to undertake the research by observation. At the time, I would have liked to combine this with interviews with the young people about their court experiences but problems with access and resources made this difficult. I was also unsure whether I, as a lawyer rather than a social scientist, had the necessary skills in this area. I have already recognized this as a limitation of the research not least given that any research that attempts to consider the perspective of young people should engage with them directly on their experiences. I think the reality though is that this can be challenging, for various reasons, and we need to acknowledge this and do it for the right reasons; I think it's particularly important to avoid tokenism.

The process of the research was relatively straightforward. I had a very small grant, from the Irish Research Council for the Humanities and Social Sciences and so the project was intended as a pilot. I undertook an initial part of the study in one court and then quickly discovered that I would have to observe as many courts as possible to give the findings some depth. It was this latter factor that gave the findings their diversity. My own interest in the area – and the willingness of my researchers to undertake much of the observation work gratis – persuaded me to expand it nationally to observation of 53 court days and nearly 1,000 cases. In the end, I observed four different courts and many more judges.

Phil Jones: How do you see the research in relation to change, young people and the justice system?

Ursula Kilkelly: The research had the objective of measuring the extent to which children are involved in Children Court proceedings. It did that and made recommendations as to how to improve the process from the child's perspective. It also considered related issues about the manner in which the Children Court operates in the Irish legal system (its adherence to statutory requirements in the Children Act 2001, for example) and in many respects highlighted, for the first time, concerns about the process in the in camera court. So, like most of my research, it was always focused on how to promote reform and to encourage change/the implementation of best practice in the way the court operates. This kind of study, although controversial, highly sensitive and very challenging, is critical to our understanding of how children are treated in the criminal process and to ensure that those who are responsible for that treatment are aware of the best practice, statutory requirements and legal obligations (national and international) that should guide their actions.

What does research reveal about the impact of new thinking and practice in relation to rights and decision making in different spaces within children's lives?

Rights-based challenges to ideas and practices, such as those cited in the previous section, have resulted in new ways of working that seek to involve children and young people in decision making. This section examines some of these by drawing on three different examples of guidelines and perspectives on decision making and rights in order to look at the ways in which more general points emerge from the specific experiences. The examples are chosen to emphasize different aspects and levels of decision making.

The Australian National Childcare Accreditation Council describes a way of working that connects rights, power and decision making and young children. They note that in a busy work environment it is easy to forget that young children are both resourceful and have the ability to contribute to their own development. They comment that adults have 'great power over children' in terms of physical strength and size, control over resources and in terms of adult power to decide over issues such as what will happen and what is fair' (www.ncac.gov.au, 2). They place their approach to work with children in a way that recognizes this but that emphasizes the importance of adults needing to see that children need to exercise their own power, to be seen as capable and to be encouraged by the messages they receive from adults that they can become competent and capable:

> Children need to have the self-confidence and skills to explore, take on new challenges, test their theories about how the world works, make mistakes and discover unexpected consequences. This self confidence is more likely to occur when children are provided with an opportunity to contribute to their own experiences and learning, sharing in decisions about what they do and how they do it.
>
> (www.ncac.gov.au/factsheets/factsheet2, 2)

Key points: ANCAC approach to decision making

- They see decision making as key to child rights, and they position it as a 'life skill' in need of time and practice to develop.
- The day care setting is seen by them as a safe environment to practice and rehearse decision making.
- This is accompanied by an assessment of the ways in which practical engagement between adults and children can foster decision making in children.
- They advocate involving young children in setting rules and boundaries in resolving everyday conflicts within the groups and encouraging decision making by support and positive feedback.
- Space and furnishings to enable children to make choices about what they do and with whom – to play with others, or alone, to be quiet or active

- Easy access to materials that allow children to obtain things they want independently, and that allow choice and decisions to match their level of competence with their play materials.

(www.ncac.gov.au/factsheets/factsheet2, 3)

Activity 1

How do you see these key points in relation to the relationship, made by ANCAC, between self-confidence, decision making and rights?

Activity 2

What models of relationship between adults and young children are reflected in the approach within the boxed key points?

On a broader, strategic level the Canadian Association for School Health (CASH), a federation of 12 provincial/territorial coalitions, promote the use the school as a strategic site within the community to reach children and youth as well as adults. It has been involved in developing five sets of criteria assessing the effectiveness of youth involvement in public decision making were developed from a variety of sources. The following gives a brief summary of the sets to illustrate this approach to looking at efficacy in developing the right to be involved in decision making:

Key points: CASH – five sets of criteria to assess youth involvement in public decision making

Each of these five sets includes several questions, derived from research, that assess the effectiveness of youth involvement programs and activities.

1. Relationship between Youth Involvement and Sponsor Organization Goals.
   a) How do the characteristics of the sponsoring organization relate to youth involvement?

2. The Nature of the Youth Involvement.
   a) How will youth participate collectively; is it episodic, developmental, structural or are various youth groups being linked together?
   b) How will each young person be involved individually?
   c) What are the roles to be assigned to young people?

3. The Processes to be Used.
   a) Are basic principles of youth participation being respected?
   b) Are barriers being addressed?

c) Are enabling factors in place?

d) Are the developmental needs of young people being met?

e) Are the young people accountable?

f) Are adults prepared to assist young people to participate?

4. How are these Criteria Applied to Different Types of Decision-Making? eg Youth Representatives on Governing Board or Regular Committees, Formal Consultations of Youth.

5. The Evidence of the Impact of Youth Involvement.

a) What evidence is there of the impact of the youth participation in the decision-making of the organization or on the youth leaders?

(McCall, 2009)

Activity 1

Review each of the five points and discuss how decision making and children's rights are present in each

Activity 2

Why do you think each are of the five is important to decision making?

Activity 3

Point 5 talks about the importance of 'impact' and evidence: why do you think this might be important to obtain?

Example of research: rights and decision making – a Norwegian perspective

Research with Norwegian pupils into rights and decision making asked the question: 'How can pupils have a greater say in decision-making?'

The research presented the findings the following proposals from the pupils:

- That we have a lesson in which the teacher writes up the pupils' views.
- If the adults try harder to understand, it will be easier for the pupils' voice to be heard.
- The teachers can set up individual appointments with pupils in the class so the pupils can give their views without fear of being laughed at.
- The teachers should ask questions more often.

The children also emphasized the teachers' cooperativeness:

- The teacher should lend a hand in improving things, but the pupils must also play their part.
- Everyone should be allowed to express their views and adults should accept that our views differ from theirs and should try to see things from our point of view.

- The teachers and (some) pupils should improve their ability to work together.
- The pupils appreciated the significance of utilising formal bodies, especially the pupils' council, municipal council, the children and young people's municipal council, and believed that they themselves should do a better job in this respect and draw in teachers to make things work better.

(Sandbaek and Hafdis Einarsson, 2008, 33)

The research feedback from the children also suggested that various forms of preparation such as free class discussions or girls' and boys' meetings were useful. The answers within the research were commented on by the researchers as according with the impressions gained from other answers in the findings: 'Children and young people were eager for more influence' (Sandbaek and Hafdis Einarsson, 2008, 33)

Reflections on the research

Activity

Reflect on the proposals from pupils reported in the research.:

How do you see these reflecting a rights perspective?

Do you consider them realistic and appropriate? How they might be implemented and what barriers might be encountered in trying to implement them?

The Social Care Institute for Excellence (SCIE) have prepared an effective guide to enabling the participation of children and young people in developing social care. Details of how to obtain the guide can be found at the end of this chapter. It emphasizes key relationships that it argues are crucial to effective engagement with the practice of children, decision making, participation and rights: these are summarized in Table 5.1.

They first emphasize the creation of an effective system or structure in order to enable young people to become active participants and then to be involved within decisions that affect them and their lives: 'Such structures include staff, resources, decision-making and planning processes' (2006, 7). They highlight decision making as a crucial factor in any attempt to engage with children and young people's participation. They conclude the following:

Even where organisations are committed to a culture of participation, they do not always change their ways of working as a result. Participation can only create change or improvement when children and young people can influence decision-making processes.

(2006, 7)

Key points: SCIE guide to participation

The guide suggests that organizations should consider the following areas of service development in order to establish effective structures that support participation:

- development of a participation strategy
- partnership working
- identification of participation champions
- provision of adequate resources for participation.

(2006, 7)

The key to achieving involvement in decision making is seen to lie in the creation of an effective system or structure. They propose that there are four elements which need to be considered to ensure that such a whole-systems approach is established:

- Culture
- Structure
- Practice
- Review

The four areas are depicted as four pieces of a jigsaw puzzle. This image usefully brings together many of the themes considered within this chapter concerning participation and child rights. It sees the development of participation not as a linear process but as an organic process that can occur in different ways within different kinds of settings. The image of a jigsaw is seen to show how each of the four elements can be considered separately, or developed to combine in particular ways.

CULTURE
The ethos of an organisation, shared by all staff and service users which demonstrates a commitment to participation

STRUCTURE
The planning, development and resourcing of participation evident in organisation's infrastructures.

PRACTICE
The ways of working, methods for involvement skills and knowledge which enable children and young people to become involved.

REVIEW
The monitoring and evaluation systems which enable an organisation to evidence change affected by participation.

STRUCTURE

CULTURE

REVIEW

PRACTICE

Jig saw puzzle image by permission of SCIE.
Source: (SCIE, 2006, 13)

They define the elements that combine to enable decision making as:

> *Culture:* the ethos of an organization, shared by all staff and service users, which demonstrates a commitment to participation.
>
> *Structure:* the planning, development and resourcing of participation evident in an organization's infrastructures.
>
> *Practice:* the ways of working, methods for involvement, skills and knowledge which enable children and young people to become involved.
>
> *Review:* the monitoring and evaluation systems which enable an organization to evidence change affected by children and young people's participation.

Activity

The Guide talks about the interrelationship of the four different elements. Reflect on these in relation to children's experiences of being within an education space such as a school, or health space such as a hospital. Consider the following:

1. How looking at an organization's *culture* might relate to changing its ways of conducting adult-child relationships (e.g. how teachers or doctors relate to children), the uses of space in terms of rules, the way it is managed or run to involve children more effectively in decision making?
2. How looking at an organization's *structure* might be necessary to change its ways of reviewing its work to involve children more effectively in decision making?
3. How looking at an organization's *practice* might relate to changing its ways of working to involve children more effectively in decision making?
4. How looking at an organization's *ways of reviewing and monitoring its work* might relate to changing practice to involve children more effectively in decision making?

Activities

The following activities are designed to help reflect back on some of the key concerns over the chapter as a whole

Chapter activity 1

Consider Anderson's comment from earlier in the chapter regarding the UNCRC, children's rights and decision making:

> The Committee has specifically stated that the rights to participation is important in ensuring a child's right to education, and child rights within

the education system: 'education must be provided in a way that . . . enables the child to express his or her views freely in accordance with article 12 (1) and to participate in school life.'

> (UN Committee on the Rights of the Child, Gen Comment No 1: The Aims of Education, CRC/GC/2001/1 (2001), para 8 (2008, 18))

How might the SCIE's four different elements – culture, structure, practice and review – help to critique and help change the practice described in the Research Example *Irish Youth Courts and Decision Making and Participation Rights in Courts* (Pages 119–25), concerning the courtrooms in Limerick, Cork and Waterford?

Chapter activity 2

Review the two examples concerning children's experiences of decision making within the UK education system (pages 126–30). Use the Canadian perspective, following CASH key points, to assess the efficacy of young people's involvement in the processes described.

CASH 3 – the processes to be used:

a. Are basic principles of youth participation being respected?
b. Are barriers being addressed?
c. Are enabling factors in place?
d. Are the developmental needs of youth being met?
e. Are the young people accountable?
f. Are adults prepared to assist young people to participate?

Do you think the Canadian perspective would see the UK ways of involving young people and children indecision making as effective?

Summary

This chapter has

- looked at the meaning of 'decision making',
- examined how ideas of 'decision making' relates to child rights,
- examined ways in which a child rights agenda challenges ideas and practices that exclude children from decision making,
- reviewed research in order to look at ideas and approached that effectively involve children and young people in decision making.

Further reading

Prout, A., Simmons, R. and Birchall, J. (2006) 'Reconnecting and extending the research agenda on children's participation: Mutual incentives and the participation chain', in Kay, E., Tisdall, M., Davis, J. M., Hill, M. and Prout, A. (eds) *Children, Young People and Social Inclusion*. Bristol: Policy Press.

Reviews process and motivations for participation, looking at research into children's participation in the context of debates about participation. The chapter looks at why people participate and how this relates to children's participation identifying and examining themes such as resources, mobilization and the dynamics of the participation process.

Australian National Childcare Accreditation Council. *ANCAC approach to decision making.* Available online at www.ncac.gov.au/factsheets2

Linked to 'Putting Children First', a simple description of decision making structures and strategies within a family day care environment

McCall, D. (2009) *Selected Case Studies of Youth Involvement in Public Decision Making.* Canadian Association for School Health (CASH).

Documents on health issues and strategies for health promotion of children and youth can be found on an abstract database available on the Internet on a subscription basis. Recent research projects undertaken by the centre include heart health, school readiness, student health indicators, nutrition, youth-led health promotion and AIDS prevention. Details: Public Health Agency of Canada at www.phac-aspc.gc.ca and Schoolfile at www.schoolfile.com

Social Care Institute for Excellence. (2006) *SCIE Guide 11: Involving Children and Young People in Developing Social Care.*

A detailed guide to enabling the participation of children and young people in developing social care, it offers organizations a framework for developing the participation of children and young people in the design, delivery and review of their services (www.scie.org.uk/publications/guides/guide11/index.asp)

Research details

Example of research: decision making and participation rights in Youth Courts

Kilkelly's research into Youth Courts within the Irish youth justice system relates to questions about the extent to which it meets international children's rights standards. The article examines the problems faced by the Court and considers its effectiveness as the central agency in the youth justice system, and in ensuring that the rights of the young people before it are vindicated.

Kilkelly, U. (2008) 'Youth courts & children's rights: The Irish experience', *Youth Justice*, 8(110), 39–56.

Example of research: rights and decision making – a Norwegian perspective

Survey connected to Norway's report to the UN on their compliance with the UNCRC in spring 2008. The Ministry of Children and Equality wished to communicate children and young people's views on growing up in Norway, seen in relation to some articles of the UN Convention. Eight municipalities were invited to obtain the views of children and young people: the Alna district of Oslo, Alta, Bjugn, Kautokeino, Lillesand, Sandnes, Skedsmo and Trondheim. NOVA was asked to provide guidance for the project and to present the results in an overall report. The survey contains information from pupils at all levels of the compulsory school system, and, in one municipality, also day care centre children – in all 1,274 children and young people. This figure includes information from minority, refugee and asylum-seeking children and children who are clients of the child welfare service or other targeted services – in all 32 children and young people.

Sandbaek, M. and Hafdis Einarsson, J. (2008) 'Children and young people report to the UN on their rights,' *NOVA Report* , 2b/08. Available online at www.reassess.no/index

A Rights Perspective on Family Life

6

Chapter Outline

Introduction and key questions	135
Is there a relationship between children, their families and rights?	136
Can the family support children's rights?	137
How do economic, social and political factors affect families in relation to rights?	139
What is the role of the state in relation to carers, children and their rights?	152
How can we understand the relationship between children, families and rights?	157
Summary	159
Further reading	160
Research details	160

Introduction and key questions

This chapter is concerned with the place of children's rights within the family. It is generally believed that the family is the best place for children to be brought up and government policies regarding the family work on the basis that families, in particular parents, will act in children's best interests. While there is an increasing awareness and emphasis in legislation of human rights, and within this of children's rights, there is unease about the discourse of rights, particularly in relation to children. Although the UK government has been criticized for failing to address children's rights issues (e.g. Marshall et al., 2008), there is increasing emphasis on how policies affecting children take account of the UN Convention (UNICEF, 2006). However, within the family, the impact is only beginning to be felt, and this is often associated with fears about decreasing the authority of parents. The role of the state in ensuring children's rights are addressed is also of concern, as criticisms of 'the nanny state' are put forward when legislation interferes with family life. This chapter considers debates that are central to these possible tensions:

- Is there a relationship between children, their families and rights?
- Can the family support children's rights?
- How do economic, social and political factors affect families in relation to rights?
- What is the role of the state in relation to carers, children and their rights?

Is there a relationship between children, their families and rights?

At the heart of this discussion is the question of the relationships that exist between child, family and the state as children need to be considered in different ways with each involving potential conflicts:

- Children as individuals
- Children as part of a family
- Children as part of society

The family is in the middle of the relationships and is meant to be supporting the child as an individual while ensuring that they develop positive relationships as part of the family and as part of society. However, each family will have a set of beliefs and values that influence their expectations of the child and their relationships. These may not be in keeping with either the principles of the UNCRC or with the expectations of state policies.

This chapter argues that within the family there are inevitable conflicts between children's growing autonomy and parental wishes and these are exacerbated by the expectations that are placed on parents and carers in today's society. Up to this point the term 'family' has been used without any further explanation, but this concept is also problematic and the value placed upon some kinds of families rather than others has been debated. The traditional view of the family of two heterosexual parents with a working father and a mother caring for the children is no longer the norm. Children may be part of very different family structures:

- Cohabiting parents
- 'Reformed' families
- Adoptive families

- Single parent families
- Families with same sex parents
- Both or no parents working
- Extended families
- Being in the care of the state – foster or institutional care.

Within this chapter the term 'family' will be used to cover any household that includes a child and the term 'carer/s' (rather than 'parent/s') will be used to identify the adult/s who have legal responsibility for the care and welfare of the child in order to cover the range of families identified above. The concern here is not to debate the relative merits of different families, but to consider the place of children's rights within the family and the complex relationships between the child, their family and the state within the context of multiple family structures.

Can the family support children's rights?

It is clear in Articles 3, 5, 9, 10, 18 and 27 of the 1989 UNCRC and Articles 8, 12 and 14 of the UN Convention of Human Rights that the primary responsibility for children's care and guidance should be with the family. The four main areas of rights in the UNCRC – survival, development, protection and participation – form the basis of what is expected, and the UNCRC emphasizes the holistic nature of the rights which shouldn't be considered in a fragmented way. While the law does not define in detail what parental responsibility is, the UK government identifies the following list of key roles in it's 'Direct Gov' information pages.

- providing a home for the child
- having contact with and living with the child
- protecting and maintaining the child
- disciplining the child
- choosing and providing for the child's education
- determining the religion of the child
- agreeing to the child's medical treatment
- naming the child and agreeing to any change of the child's name
- accompanying the child outside the United Kingdom and agreeing to the child's emigration, should the issue arise
- being responsible for the child's property
- appointing a guardian for the child, if necessary
- allowing confidential information about the child to be disclosed.

(Directgov at www.direct.gov.uk/en/Parents/ParentsRights/DG_4002954)

Key points: UK government's position on rights and parental roles

The list of responsibilities can be linked with the key areas of children's rights to draw out where the government's priorities might lie.

Type of right	Role of parent
Provision – survival	• providing a home for the child • protecting and maintaining the child • agreeing to the child's medical treatment
Provision – development	• having contact with and living with the child • disciplining the child • choosing and providing for the child's education • determining the religion of the child • agreeing to the child's medical treatment • determining the religion of the child
Protection	• protecting and maintaining the child • accompanying the child outside the United Kingdom and agreeing to the child's emigration, should the issue arise • being responsible for the child's property • appointing a guardian for the child, if necessary • allowing confidential information about the child to be disclosed • disciplining the child
Participation	There is no indication that parents have any duty to support children's participation

It is interesting that this list doesn't mention children's participation and that there are two major instances where child participation is actually denied. It gives those with parental responsibility the authority to determine the religion of the child and to choose their education, both of which are crucial decisions concerning the child's life about which she or he will have some view. This is indicative of the potential conflict between participation rights and protection rights and the difficulty those with parental responsibility have in balancing these. While it isn't explicitly included in the list of responsibilities, there is also an implicit expectation that it is the responsibility of carers to prepare children for their place in society, commonly referred to as 'socialization'. It is evident from the list that the government considers 'disciplining the child' as important in socialization. There is the possibility of that discipline impinging on children's rights to be protected when physical punishment is used. There are good reasons for expecting that the family is the best place for socialization to occur, and to assume that children's rights are upheld within the family. However, as well as the tensions referred to here, there are further concerns about how well the family is able to support children's rights and these will be considered in the next section.

How do economic, social and political factors affect families in relation to rights?

The context of family life has been, and is still, changing. One of the main changes is the nature of the family. The list of different family types at the beginning of the chapter indicates this change and during the period of childhood an individual child may experience more than one family form and the change this involves affects children's experiences. In addition, in Western societies there are a number of factors that affect children and their families.

- The consumer society
- Over and under employment
- Relative poverty
- The commodification of children as social and emotional assets
- The perception of danger and blame

Prout (2000) identifies the 'emergence of consumption (particularly leisure) as a source of identity' (2000, 307) as a significant change that has affected family life. Individuals and families are increasingly under pressure to purchase, leading to families needing to have more than one income in order to 'keep up' with the pressure to consume and what Jensen (2003) terms 'over employment'. In contrast, families with unemployed parents suffer not only from lack of income but also lack of status that goes along with having the right kind of possessions. Wade and Smart (2003) also identify the 'commodification of children' as part of this emphasis on materialism. As families have fewer children the importance of the child in the family has grown in being a resource that gives pleasure to parents socially and emotionally. This makes the process of separation or divorce (as part of the changing nature of families) very difficult as both parents are likely to want to maintain 'possession' of the child.

The current culture of 'blame' encourages carers to respond in particular ways to every possible danger for children. These dangers are not only physical but also emotional, social and sexual, coming in the form of unsupervised environments, strangers, media (particularly the Internet) and association with peers. All of these potential dangers are likely to be attractions to enquiring young people so they increase the potential conflict between child and carer, as the carer attempts to fulfil the expectations of protecting their child through enforcing their authority.

In contrast, within economically developing societies pressures on children and families are less likely to be as a result of the growing consumer society, and much more likely to be in relation to

- absolute poverty
- children being economic assets
- ear and political repression.

In these societies the difficulty of earning enough money to provide food and shelter for the whole family may mean that children are engaged either in paid work where they may well be exploited, or in tasks that contribute to the household such as looking after siblings or being involved in agricultural activities to provide food. This may have an effect on their access to education, play and leisure, as these become less important when the basics of life are difficult to obtain.

Although the difficulties for families in ensuring children's rights are met are very different in these different contexts, there are issues for all families. The next section considers some of the problems that emerge from relying on the family as the basis for ensuring children's rights are upheld.

Provision rights

The Children's Society (2009) found that most children said that parental love, care support, respect and fairness (2009, 4) were important things about being in a family and form the basis of most family relationships. However, Engle (2006) points to the discrimination that takes place in some families because of gender, disability, birth order and physical attractiveness, and it would also be possible to add sexuality to this list. In these cases parental attitudes to particular children may be such that the love, emotional security and affective support are lacking. Even when these basics exist, some families have difficulty making provision for children because of their lack of financial resources and this can impact on children's lives in many ways.

Example of research: the effects of poverty

In reviewing the literature on the effects of poverty in industrialized countries Griggs and Walker (2008) found the following:

- Poverty impacts on children's self-confidence and their relationships with other children.
- Young people living in low-income households report a stigma attached to their circumstances, and feel at risk from exclusion and bullying which, in turn, impacts on school and community involvement.
- Some children feel embarrassed about their impoverished circumstances, particularly when a lack of money means they are unable to participate in social activities.
- Children growing up in poverty are more likely to suffer from low self-esteem, to feel that they are 'useless' or 'a failure' and to be socially isolated.

Reflection on research

As well as 'relative poverty' the earlier list of factors affecting families included 'consumer society'.

Activity

How do you think that pressures to wear the 'right' sort of clothes, own the 'right' sort of technology and engage in the 'right' sort of activities might contribute to the effects of relative poverty described in this research?

These effects are largely social and emotional, but these feelings of exclusion and low self-esteem are very likely to have an impact on other areas of development. Children may go on to have difficulty in relationships, have poor academic achievement and become involved in anti-social activities, all affecting children's rights to development. However, in countries where levels of poverty are even greater, often because of conflict, families have difficulty providing for even the most basic rights.

The following extract from Save the Children's 'Personal Stories' webpage shows the impact of the post election conflict in Kenya on one family. Maria is 13 and lives in Nairobi:

They came into my house and started to loot everything and told us we had to leave. I felt bad and was frightened. We left everything in our house when we fled – we came here with nothing. We have been in the camp for three weeks. We came here with my mother.

> They say everyone must leave tomorrow – I don't know where we can go. I would like to stay here. I am afraid that if we go to a new place to live that people will start fighting again.
>
> We learn in the tents here and have a kind of school. I love studying English. I want to go to school but people say that if we go they will burn it. They did not get peace so they say that if the schools open they will burn them.

Maria's family are virtually powerless to provide for her in this situation and the effects of this absolute level of poverty are likely to be more immediate than the effects of relative poverty described by Griggs and Walker.

Key points: the family and provision rights

The family's ability to provide for children's rights to survival and development are affected by

- absolute and relative poverty,
- armed conflict

and the effects of these can be made worse by the emphasis on consumerism in industrialized countries.

Protection rights

Within economically developed countries difficulties of protecting children within families mainly stem from two areas:

- Pressures on parents to protect children from outside influences with the possibility that this leads to overprotection,
- Abuse that takes place within the family.

Overprotection

The UK Children's Commissioners' report identified

> there is evidence of an over-protective attitude towards children that reduces their opportunities for play, leisure, recreation and healthy development. This may be fuelled by parental fears or by institutional avoidance of any risk that might lead to liability. In Scotland, research has shown that adults fear contact with children in case they are accused of

harming a child. This very wide-spread and significant fear has created an unhealthy climate that limits opportunities and hampers development.

(Marshall et al., 2008, 7)

These fears of external dangers are real: children can be in danger from such things as increased traffic, people who may harm them, exposure to images and 'grooming' on the Internet and media images and pressures. However, to live in a risk-free environment is impossible.

Activity

Can you think of some of the restrictions that parents might put on a child because of this type of fear? What effects might this have in the short term? What effects might it have in the longer term?

While the fear of strangers and the harm that they might cause children is widespread, the most likely source of harm from adults comes from within the family. The term 'abuse' within the family usually refers to physical and sexual abuse, but exactly what constitutes abuse is difficult to define. Instances of abuse within families are diagnosed as being pathological: not what 'normal families' engage in. One specific contentious area of potential abuse is smacking and, as this is still legal within the United Kingdom, it isn't seen as abnormal behaviour.

Example of research: what do we mean by 'abuse'?

Mason and Falloon (2001) researched the views of children in Australia on what they thought constituted abuse. They found that the children identified a number of features that they associated with abuse:

- The emotional as well as the physical aspects of abuse, for example, 'like someone getting to you from your insides, like shredding something that really matters to you'.
- The abuse of the unequal power relationships between adults and children e.g. 'because you're not allowed to smack anyone else but children . . . I can't smack.'
- The fear of disclosing abuse and the children's limited agency: 'you and your parents have been like together and they support you and if you, if maybe you go against them then they'll go against you and you've got no-one to support you.'

Reflection on the research

What these children are referring to in the first two instances is beyond the scope of what is identified as abuse in legal cases. As such, Mason and Falloon believe that we shouldn't see abuse as being pathological but as something that takes place in all families to some degree because of the power relationships between parents and children.

⇨

Activity 1
What is your response to this point of view concerning abuse in families?

Activity 2
Perceiving abuse in this way would suggest that families have difficulty in protecting children. How would relationships between children and their parents need to change to avoid the abuse that the children in the research identified?

In contrast to these ideas of how children in economically developed countries need to be protected, we should also consider the experiences of children in circumstances of extreme poverty and the difficulties that families face in protecting them.

Research example: poverty and child labour

Save the Children (2007) reported on the extent of child labour across the world and identify how family poverty can lead to eight particular forms of child slavery

- child trafficking,
- commercial sexual exploitation,
- bonded child labour,
- forced work in mines,
- forced agricultural labour,
- child soldiers/combatants,
- forced child marriage,
- domestic slavery.

One of the areas they report on is bonded child labour where the report describes how their parents take out a loan to pay for their home, medicine or maybe just food. They are then obliged to work for the money-lender in lieu of the money. The whole family, including children, must work until they have effectively paid back the money. This can take years for even the smallest amount. These bonded workers have no power to negotiate the repayment rate or the interest added to the original sum. Unable to earn money of their own, parents are often forced to take out further loans, increasing the amount they owe.

They found that

- In Nepal, there are approximately 200,000 bonded labourers, many of them children.
- In Pakistan's Sind province, almost seven million bonded labourers, including children, work for their landlords without pay.
- Around 250,000 children live and work in Pakistani brick kilns in complete social isolation.

⇨

Reflections on research

In all these situations children are being exploited: they are not working out of choice and they are not working in conditions where they are protected. The reason that they can be exploited in these ways is because their families are unable to protect them: their work may be the only means of keeping the family alive.

Activity

In concluding their report Save the Children asks the public to

- lobby their MPs to make the elimination of child slavery a priority,
- support fair trade initiatives that protect the rights of child labourers.

How do you think these things might make a difference to the lives of these children? What would be needed to enable the families to protect their children?

Key points: the family and protection rights

- The circumstances of families in economically developed and developing countries are very different and lead to different issues for the family in protecting children.
- In economically developed countries attempts to protect children from external hazards may lead to situations where children's freedoms are restricted unnecessarily.
- Definitions of what constitutes 'abuse' affect the experiences of children in families.
- Absolute poverty and armed conflict affect the family's capacity to protect children from exploitation.

Participation rights

Within the family the assumption is that parents will automatically put children's 'best interests' first but their powerful position in relation to their children and the demands that are made of them externally make this a difficult thing to do. Although putting forward a case against children's agency rights, Brighouse (2002) points out that the Human Rights Convention puts forward the responsibilities that exist when there are power differentials between individuals.

> You may indeed have superior power but this fact does not authorise you to use your power to your own advantage. In some cases you must attempt to relinquish this power. But in others, when it cannot be relinquished, you must understand

> that the person in your power is a rights-bearer, one whose interests count for as much as yours. When you use your power with respect to that person you are morally bound to attend first to their, and only after to your own, interests.
>
> (Brighouse, 2002, 36)

When put against the concept of 'the child's best interests' this makes it clear that carers need to be aware of the power relationship that they have with the child and acknowledge that their personal interests may be in conflict with the child's. Knowing the child's thoughts on the matter can only be beneficial in trying to make the best decision.

The main implication of these ideas is that in order for carers to act in the best interests of the child they need to be aware of and respect the views of the child. This doesn't mean that the child will always do exactly what he or she wants but he or she will participate in discussions about what actions might be best. Interestingly, Thomas's (2000) research into children's participation in decision making found that 'what they wanted was above all the opportunity to take part in dialogue with adults, not for either themselves or the adults to determine the outcome' (2000, 152) Perhaps this finding might alleviate concerns from carers about losing authority unless they consider that 'authority' means acting in their own interests rather than the child's. The economic dependence that children and young people in economically developed countries have on their families and the constraints on their time and use of space because of the fear of danger are likely to affect the negotiating position of children in the family. However, when children are more involved in the family's economic welfare this may give them more scope for negotiation.

Example of research: rights, work and agency

Punch (2001) researched the lives of children in rural Bolivia where 'children are expected to work and are active contributors to the household from a very young age.'

This gives them a degree of mobility within the community that is rare for children in economically developed societies and they are away from adult surveillance. She argues that this enables them to be part of a 'complex process in which they assert their agency, creating time and space for themselves despite restrictions from a variety of sources, including adults, other children and structural constraints.'

The following is an example of a child–parent negotiation where mother (Dolores) and eldest daughter (Marienela, 10 years) share many of the domestic duties; in this case, Dolores wants Marienela to make the half-hour walk each way to take her father his lunch.

> Marienela: I'm not going to go.
> Dolores: Now you have to go. Can't you take my place for just one day?
> Marienela: No I can't
> Dolores: But I always do it during the week.

The result was that Dolores took the lunch but on condition that Marienela looked after her 2-year-old brother and kept an eye on the animals.

Reflection on research

This is a good illustration of children not being able to do what they want but being able to take part in the decision making of the family as a serious participant.

Activity

What do you think Marienela is learning about her status in the family and the interdependence of all family members?

One area that is potentially very difficult for families is respecting children's autonomy in matters of culture and religion. The UNCRC identifies the child's right to their own religion and culture and this is generally interpreted as being that of their parents. Indeed the European Convention on Human Rights identifies the rights of parents to bring up their child in accordance with their religious beliefs. The difficulty lies in doing this in such a way that it allows the child to be able to develop their own views at some stage without being under pressure to follow the culture or religion of their family.

Example of research: rights, families and religion

Horwath et al. (2008) researched the views of parents and children about religion and found that

> most parents saw religion as a way of life that was transmitted between generations. They considered it part of their parenting responsibility to pass on their faith.

> Although young people understood that formal worship could be an important shared activity in religious families and a duty for some of their parents, most thought they should not be forced to attend.

They also found that

> parents acknowledged that as children grew up they had to make their own choices about their beliefs. However, there were differing views about the age at which young people could make informed choices, including whether to engage in religious activities. . . . Although some young people and parents from different faith groups claimed religious authority for strict views on issues such as sex outside marriage and homosexuality, parents often seemed more measured and tolerant about these issues than young people anticipated. More generally, young people and parents considered it was crucial that parents, from early childhood, begin to provide young people with the skills to resist external pressures on their religious way of life and choices.

Reflection on research

In this research parents acknowledge that when the child becomes an adult he or she should be able to make decisions about religion but are unsure what age that should be.

The research paints quite a positive view of parent–child relationships around religion, but there are issues concerning the difficult line between informing children about the religion of the parents and pressurizing them into conformity. The parents and children in the research thought it crucial for parents to provide young people with strategies to resist external pressures.

Activity 1
Do you think it is possible to bring a child up to believe in a religion in such a way that they are open minded enough at a later date to reject that religion?

Activity 2
A person's identity and culture are often closely linked with religion. How might rejecting the religion of your family have an impact on someone's sense of identity and their sense of belonging to a community?

Interview with Jan Horwath about her research

Jan Horwath, Professor in Child Welfare, Department of Sociological Studies, University of Sheffield

Sue Welch: How do you see the findings of your research in relation to children's participation rights?

Jan Horwath: This study drew on the views of 74 young people living in England aged between 13–15 years who represented five faith traditions. The findings from the study highlighted that in order to promote active participation of young people in society it is important to recognize the influence of religious beliefs and practices on the ways in which young people wish to conduct their lives. In order to achieve this it is important to understand, as highlighted by the findings of the study, that young people hold a diverse range of beliefs and practices; from those who believe in a God but do not engage in religious practices through to those who both believe and actively engage in a faith community. In addition some young people and their parents adopt a pick and mix approach taking aspects of their religion that fit with their own values and beliefs.

In order to promote the rights of young people holding religious beliefs the findings from the study would indicate it is important to consider how these beliefs influence their daily life and life choices. For example, amongst this sample religious beliefs influenced the choices young people made about dress, listening to music, selecting friends and choosing a career. The participants recognized the pressures placed on young people from peers, the media and mainstream adolescent culture to make choices which may not necessarily fit with the family's religious beliefs and practices. This was evident in relation to sexual relationships and can raise issues regarding the young person's right to engage in sex before marriage or same-sex relationships if these activities go against the teaching of their particular faith. The young people and parents considered it was crucial that parents, from early childhood, begin to provide young people with the skills to manage these situations. Both parents and young people in the study acknowledged that as children grow up they have to make their own choices about their religious beliefs and practices. This can be informed by influences outside the family such as peers. However, it is important that the rights of young people to select their own values and beliefs should be respected.

Sue Welch: What did you discover about further directions for research from this experience?

Jan Horwath: This study focused on the perceptions of young people regarding the influence of religious beliefs on parenting and adolescent life. It would, therefore, be valuable to build on this research to study how religion actually influences daily life experiences and life choices. Moreover the study targeted 13–15-year-olds. When the young people and their parents discussed topics such as sexual relationships they focused on how they believed they would manage the situation, on occasion making reference to real-life examples. This would be worth pursuing further in a study of older adolescents and young adults which focuses on how members of this age group who hold religious beliefs manage some of the tensions around balancing the norms in society against the teachings of their faith as described in this study. Finally, a comparative study of adolescents and parents from atheist, humanist and agnostic backgrounds would be valuable to identify if the values and beliefs held by those with religious beliefs towards parenting adolescents are that different.

An Illustration of these possible tensions can be found in a small-scale research project undertaken by a group of young South Asians living in Kirklees that identified the 'double life' that some young people have to negotiate between their family life and life outside the family.

Example of research: leading a double life within and outside the family

Ahmad et al. worked with 36 young people between the ages of 11 and 21 to identify their experience of living with two different cultures.

They found that while all the young people identified with the concept of a 'double life' 30 per cent felt they were trapped between the culture of their family and modern, Western society. Some examples of the comments made are:

> My parents tell me to pray everyday five times a day but I don't want to.

> Quite possibly with regards to marriage/marriage partners, clothes, education and work opportunities. Parents may want their children to act according to their culture and religion, while some South Asian Young people may not feel as much obliged to follow their culture, religion and family compared to their parents and may feel more inclined to the western society.

Equally they felt under pressure to conform to the accepted behaviour of the Western culture that they met outside the home, for example,

> Yes, it can, a person could be pressured by friends, and it can be hard to say no as don't want to be left out.

> Yes, because mates might want you to do something that you don't want to do.

> Yes, because it is difficult to say no to friends because then they start back biting so you follow because you don't want that, you want to be like every body else.

> Yes, they could be forced into smoking, boyfriends when you don't want to.

> Yes, because friends might force you to do something against your religion and culture.

Unfortunately many of the young people felt unable to talk to their family about the difficulties because of the following:

> Feel being judged

> Fear of parents

> Family might tell parents

> Might have the fear of getting hit by parents

> Feel they don't connect

Generation gap

Blackmailing by family, brothers and sisters

Culture and religion – you have to have two different personalities to be able to cope with life today.

As a result, the researchers identified a need for professional support for young people in this situation to help them to explore these conflicts and how to deal with them and made the following recommendations:

There is a need to educate professionals on cultural and religious issues and needs:

- Services need to meet the health and emotional well-being needs of South Asian young people through specialist services being developed.
- Appropriate service development for young people from Asian communities requires their involvement in planning and implementation from the outset, rather than attempting to slot them into services that are not tailored to meet their needs.
- Professionals from schools, education, health and social services need to understand how ideas of parenting, childhood and 'youth' differ not only between ethnic groups but also within each sub ethnic group.
- Undertaking further evaluation and research with this group of young people with a focus on young South Asian males.
- Local authorities need to identify the cultural and social needs of this group in strategic documentation and identify clear needs.

Reflection on research

The results of this research emphasize more of the difficulties that young South Asians face than the previous research summary. This was a smaller scale study and was carried out by researchers who were young South Asians themselves.

Activity

How do you think this might have affected the findings?

The perceptions of adult professionals was included but not the perceptions of parents.

Why do you think this might have been the case?

Although this research concentrated on young people from a culture that might be seen as very different from a Western culture, the same kinds of difficulties might be experienced by children whose families have any strong beliefs about religion or culture.

> ### Key points: families and participation
>
> - Children's ability to participate in decisions within the family depends on the kinds of relationships that exist between family members. This may be influenced by the economic status of the child.
> - Carers have a very difficult task in enabling children to develop their own identity and beliefs while giving them the security of belonging within a family and community with its own culture and beliefs.

What is the role of the state in relation to carers, children and their rights?

The role of the state in family matters was at the heart of the opposition to ratification of the UNCRC in the United States. Their reasons for opposing the convention are that 'the best interests of the child' and 'the evolving capacities of children' will lead to the state, through the courts of law, deciding what these mean rather than parents (Parental Rights, 2008). This objection sees state intervention as interference in family life and has parallels with arguments about liberty rights that were discussed in Chapter 2. Archard (1993) explores this concern and identifies the 'liberal standard' that considers parents and carers know what is best for their children and have a right to bring up their children as they think fit. In this case the state should not interfere unless the child is in danger. He goes on to identify three elements:

- Commitment to the importance of 'the best interests of the child'.
- Parent and carers have the right to autonomy (freedom to bring up their children as they see fit) and privacy (no one can intrude in the family without consent).
- There are clear conditions that identify when it is appropriate for the state to intervene.

Within UK culture the last of these elements is usually in relation to children suffering abuse or neglect. When there is sufficient evidence that a child is 'at risk of significant harm' and the 'best interests' of the child are in danger, the state can interfere with the parents' or carers' rights to privacy and autonomy. However, the assumption explicit in The Children Act 1989 is that the best place for a child to be is with their family.

The state and provision

In contrast to the liberal standard there is an expectation in the UNCRC that the state has a more positive role in supporting parents and carers in making adequate provision for their children. Fiscal policy, education services, welfare benefits and health and social services are all forms of state intervention but are generally seen as being there to support parents and carers in upholding children's provision rights. However, state provision is often influenced by political considerations that are as concerned with appearing to be tough on those who don't fit 'the norm' and economic prudence as with supporting children's rights to adequate support. This can lead to policies that appear to be supporting the child within the family setting but in reality have more negative outcomes.

Example of research: time poverty and income poverty

Burchardt (2008) identified the importance of time poverty as well as income poverty. She points out that, while some parents work long hours in order to provide a good standard of living for their family, this may result in 'time poverty' where they don't have time to spend with their children. For many of these families there would be an option of reducing working time in order to have more time to spend with their children. She was particularly interested in those families who had to work long hours in order to provide a basic standard of living and who would fall into poverty if they reduced their working hours. For these families the choice was between being 'time poor' or being 'income poor': there wasn't any other option. She researched the effects of policy on these families and found that around half (between 42 and 56 per cent, depending on the poverty definition used) of lone parents are not in a position to generate sufficient income to be above an income poverty line while still meeting basic obligations (e.g. to ensure their children are looked after, by themselves or someone else), however long or hard they work.

She concludes that the government's welfare reform and child poverty agendas risk freeing lone parents from income poverty only at the price of deepening their existing time poverty.

Reflections on research

Activity

What do you think this says about the state's attitude to lone parents?

What could policy makers do to support lone parents in a way that would ensure that they have both the time and money to support their children?

How would this be funded?

What objections would be raised by those who believe that the state has a minimal role to play in family life?

The state and protection

Protecting children from the actions of their parents and carers is probably the most controversial aspect of the relationship between families and the state. The very fine line between too little and too much 'interference' means that children may die through the actions of their carers or may be taken from their carers unnecessarily. The judgements that have to be made in cases of suspected physical and sexual abuse are extremely difficult as the following two cases illustrate.

In 1987 in Cleveland two paediatricians diagnosed sexual abuse in 121 children from 57 families in the area. Most of the children were removed from their homes under place of safety orders. At the end of the enquiry 96 of the children were returned to their parents as there wasn't sufficient evidence of abuse. The media coverage at the time and afterwards pointed to the over-protective approach by paediatricians and social workers although an enquiry by Lady Butler-Sloss pointed to the deficiencies in the process rather than the judgements of individuals as being at the heart of the problem.

Whatever the causes were, there was considerable trauma caused to the children and families involved.

In 2003 Lord Laming reported on his investigation into the case of Victoria Climbie in order to find out 'why this once happy, smiling, enthusiastic little girl – brought to this country by a relative for "a better life" – ended her days the victim of almost unimaginable cruelty.' The horror of what happened to her during her last months was captured by Counsel to the Inquiry, Neil Garnham QC, who told the Inquiry:

> The food would be cold and would be given to her on a piece of plastic while she was tied up in the bath. She would eat it like a dog, pushing her face to the plate. Except, of course that a dog is not usually tied up in a plastic bag full of its excrement. To say that Kouao and Manning treated Victoria like a dog would be wholly unfair; she was treated worse than a dog.
>
> On 12 January 2001, Victoria's great-aunt, Marie-Therese Kouao, and Carl John Manning were convicted of her murder.
>
> (Laming, 2003, 1)

In Cleveland the professionals involved were accused of too much interference but in the Victoria Climbie case they were accused of non-intervention.

Although the cases were very different and the complexity of each case isn't covered here, the issues of the relationship between the state and the family is at the heart of them both.

This difficult relationship between the role of the state in supporting families and protecting children was part of a research report, The Children Act Now: messages from research (Aldgate and Statham, 2001). The findings indicated that it may be possible for these difficulties to be addressed through listening to those involved.

Key points: relationships between family and state

Research into parental response to services across a range of provision found that parents wanted:

- services that are targeted at the whole family, not just the child;
- interagency services that are well co-ordinated;
- services that offer a combination of practical and emotional help;
- services that are offered in a welcoming, non-stigmatizing manner;
- family centres that combine referred and non-referred cases and offer open access to a range of services or activities;
- transparency about the purpose and expected outcomes of services; and
- social workers who are approachable, honest, understanding, reliable, helpful and have time to listen.

Aldgate and Statham, 2001: 81

The state and participation

Since ratification of the UNCRC children's participation rights have gradually been given more consideration through the 1989 Children Act and, more recently, the 2004 Children Act. However, the state does not intervene in children's participation rights within the family unless there is a dispute between parents, as in divorce cases. As Qvortrup et al. (1994) point out, the needs of parents/carers and children are often seen as indivisible in the services that are provided by the state: so the relationship that the state has with children is nearly always through the family. This 'familialization' (Qvortrup et al., 1994) may account for the State's apparent lack of concern in children's participation rights within the family. Brannen and O'Brien (1996) suggest that this means that children are 'conceptually constrained by and substantively contained within, the social institutions of family and school' (1996, 1). The need for children to have a more direct relationship with services provided by the state is illustrated in the following example.

Example of research: participation and protection

Research by Gorin (2004) for the Joseph Rowntree Foundation, identifies how children who are living in families where parents have some sort of mental health problem are often ignored in discussions about their parents.

She found that children wanted to be informed about their parent's problems in a way that they could understand and gave the following illustration:

> People tend to protect children and young people. For me, this translated into ignoring my need to be informed and involved. My life was affected anyway and if I had guidance it might have made the experience more positive. I needed good, age-specific information about my mother's condition and its consequences. And I needed someone to talk to who would listen in confidence and help me to express and explore the complex feelings and situations I was dealing with.
>
> (Marlowe [1996], cited in Gorin, 2004).

Reflections on the research

The research highlights the difficulties in balancing children's rights to be protected with their rights to be informed and participate in decisions that affect them. The social worker is likely to have the parent as his or her main focus and may feel that the child needs to be protected from the realities of their parent's problems.

Activity

Look at the key points in the previous box. These were concerned with the relationship between family and state but may also be applicable in this case. Go through the points and think about how the child in this research might have benefited from their application.

The role of the Children's Commissioner was intended to provide a more direct link between the state and children, but in England the role has been criticized for being 'weak', 'lacking a rights focus' and being 'under political control' in comparison to equivalent roles in other regions within the United Kingdom (Wise, 2004).

The main fears concerning the role of the state centre on children's participation rights and how the legal system might override parental decisions. Many of the concerns about children's provision and protection rights involve decisions being made by parents and carers 'in the best interests of the child'. Without the involvement of children themselves in making those decisions it is unlikely that parents and carers can really determine what is in the child's best interests so participation rights become central to ensuring other rights too.

Although the UK government hasn't incorporated children's participation rights within the family into its laws there are countries that have. Thomas (2000) identifies Scotland, Norway and Sweden as countries where these rights are incorporated in law and points out that the fears about increased litigation in response to doing this haven't materialized. However, by emphasizing the potential conflict between children's and carer's rights, the prospect of litigation might be increased. Arneil (2002) suggests a possible alternative model. She argues that an individual rights dialogue based on liberal notion of rights may not be helpful to the child or carers and considers that more emphasis on our interdependence would create a less confrontational context. Thomas (2000) echoes this notion when he argues that 'How can we live together?' is a better question than 'Why should I not do exactly as I want?' as a basis for negotiating rights.

However, the current position is one where adults, and within the family, carers, have power over children. Our current society also views children as 'adults in the making' which reinforces this power differential between adults and children. Thomas (2000) questions whether adults will be willing to relinquish this power in order to acknowledge our interdependence and seek to find ways of living together.

How can we understand the relationship between children, families and rights?

This chapter has considered the challenges that face families in economically developed and developing countries in supporting children's rights. It is clear that the extent to which children can be provided for and protected within their family depends on the family's economic, social and cultural circumstances and that the degree of child participation in decision making is influenced by the relationships within the family and the perceived status of children. These circumstances can be affected both positively and negatively by the policies and practices of the state through the services that they provide.

The tensions between welfare rights and liberty rights that were highlighted in Chapter 2 are paralleled in the relationships that exist between children and their families and children, families and state.

In relation to children and families there is a tension between how parents and carers protect and provide for children (welfare rights) while ensuring children participate as fully as possible in decisions that are made (liberty rights). The state can take a positive role in providing services that support the family's ability to provide for and protect children. However, in doing so they may be seen to be taking away some of the autonomy that parents and carers have. This relationship between family and state becomes particularly problematic when children's participation rights are concerned as the relationship between the state and the child is usually mediated by the family. However, those working with children and families do have the opportunity to support all children's rights by ensuring that they listen and take into account the views of children and other family members in finding ways to provide for children's survival and development and protect them from exploitation and harm. If the relationship between the state and the family models the good practice of involving and negotiating ways forward, the possibility of changing relationships within the family to give children a position of respect where they are part of the decision making process is far more likely.

Activities

The following activities are designed to help reflect back on some of the key concerns over the chapter as a whole:

Chapter activity 1

The chapter discusses the UK government's position as reflected in its guidance to parents on their responsibilities and notes that the responsibilities are largely in relation to ensuring children are socialized into the values of society and are provided for and protected. It goes on to say,

> It is interesting that this list doesn't mention children's participation and there are 2 major instances where child participation is denied. It gives

those with parental responsibility the authority to determine the religion of the child and choose their education, both of which are crucial decisions concerning the child's life about which s/he will have some view.

Review the list on page 138 and consider

a. why you think these omissions occur, and
b. what you think a different position might be concerning parents, children's rights and
    Parental authority to determine the religion of a child
    Parental authority to choose the education of a child.

In particular discuss factors such as age, maturity, power and culture in your analysis.

Chapter activity 2

The chapter draws on Archard's influential commentary on rights in relation to the following:

- Commitment to the importance of 'the best interests of the child'.
- Parent and carers have the right to autonomy (freedom to bring up their children as they see fit) and privacy (no one can intrude in the family without consent).
- There are clear conditions that identify when it is appropriate for the state to intervene.

Consider the issue of the state's position of the 'best interests' of a child being made by parents or adults working with children in relation to the research by Gorin on page 156.

How do children's rights relate to their involvement or non-involvement in decisions made about the services they receive?

Summary

This chapter has

- examined the relationship between children, their families and rights;
- looked at how the family can support children's rights;
- considered how economic, social and political factors affect families in relation to rights;
- examined the role of the state in relation to carers, children and their rights;
- considered the relationship between children, their families and rights.

Further reading

Archard, D. (1993) *Children: Rights and Childhood*. London: Routledge.

Chapter 9, 'Family and State', explains the different philosophical positions regarding the relationship between the family and the state and how these influence ideas about children's rights within the family.

The Children's Society (2009) *The Good Childhood Enquiry: What Children Told Us*. Available on at
  www.childrenssociety.org.uk/resources/documents/good%20childhood/14690_full.pdf

This large-scale research project collected evidence from children and this paper summarizes what the children in the research think about being part of a family.

Thomas, N. (2000) *Children, Family and the State: Decision-Making and Child Participation*. London:
  Macmillan.

Chapter 5, 'Children, Parents and the State', considers the kind of relationships between parents and children that need to exist in order to support children's rights.

Research details

Example of research: the effects of poverty

The report funded by the Joseph Rowntree Foundation reviews evidence on the impact of poverty for individuals growing up in industrialized, OECD (Organization for Economic Cooperation and Development) countries. It uses a conceptual framework to explore how child poverty has short-, medium- and long-term consequences for individuals, families, neighbourhoods and society/the economy. These consequences relate to health, education, employment, behaviour, finance, relationships and subjective well-being.

Griggs, J. and Walker, R. (2008) *The Costs of Child Poverty for Individuals and Society: A Literature
  Review*. York: Joseph Rowntree Foundation.

Example of research: what do we mean by 'abuse'?

The research is reported as a chapter in a book on child–adult relationships. The qualitative research was based on focus group discussions with mainstream young people in Sydney. The researchers paid attention to four imperatives for researching 'silenced' groups in order to identify the views of the young people on abuse.

Mason, J. and Falloon, J. (2001) 'Some Sydney children define abuse: Implications for agency in childhood', in Alanen, L. and Mayall, B. (eds) *Conceptualizing Child-Adult Relations*. London: Routledge/
  Falmer.

Example of research: poverty and child labour

The report for Save the Children draws on the work of Save the Children and other partner organizations to identify the experiences of children in various kinds of forced labour.

Save the Children. (2007) *The small hand of slavery*. London: Save the Children. Available online at www.savethechildren.org.uk/en/docs/child_slavery_briefing.pdf

Example of research: rights, work and agency

Punch carried out an ethnographic study of the daily lives of children in Bolivia and how they negotiate autonomy. A sample of 18 households were visited regularly to carry out semi-structured and informal interviews and semi-participant observations. Classroom observations and a variety of task-based techniques were used in school.

Punch, S. (2001) 'Negotiating autonomy: Childhoods in rural Bolivia', in Alanen, L. and Mayall, B. (eds) *Conceptualizing Child-Adult Relations*. London: Routledge/Falmer.

Example of research: rights, families and religion

The research funded by the Joseph Rowntree Foundation investigated the effects of religion on parenting by using focus group discussions. Forty young people aged between 13 and 15 years from 6 schools participated in these groups. Similar discussions took place with parents unrelated to the young people in the focus groups.

Horwath, J., Lees, J., Sidebotham, P., Higgins, J. and Imitiaz, A. (2008) *Religion, Beliefs and Parenting Practices*. York: Joseph Rowntree Foundation. Available online at www.jrf.org.uk/bookshop/eBooks/2264-faith-parenting-youth.pdf

Example of research: leading a double life within and outside the family

Ahmad et al. worked with 36 young people between the ages of 11 and 21 to identify their experience of living with two different cultures. The researchers were young people themselves and the research was supported by the Young Researchers' Network and Barnardos.

Ahmad, S. Akbar, A. Akbar, H. Ayub, S. Batool, A. Batool, S., Hussain, B. Kiani, S. Mahmood, S. and Rauf, R. (2008) 'East meets West – Why do some South Asian young people feel they need to lead a double identity and how does cultural and religious issues affect them', *Young Researchers Network*. Available online at childrens-research-centre.open.ac.uk/research/Barnardo'sresearchreport.pdf

Example of research: time poverty and income poverty

This research supported by the Joseph Rowntree Foundation used a small number of semi-structured interviews with people who were juggling work and family responsibilities and who felt under both time and income pressure. These were followed up after two years. Quantitative analysis of national statistics gave information about people's daily and weekly activities and economic and family circumstances.

Burchardt, T. (2008) 'Time and income poverty', *CASE Report 57*. London: London School of Economics. Available online at http://sticerd.lse.ac.uk/dps/case/cr/CASEreport57.pdf

Example of research: participation and protection

Gorin's literature review draws together research findings about children's experiences of living with domestic violence, parental substance misuse (drugs and alcohol) and parental health problems.

Gorin, S. (2004) *Understanding What Children Say: Children's Experiences of Domestic Violence, Parental Substance Misuse and Parental Health Problems*. York: Joseph Rowntree Foundation. Available online at www.jrf.org.uk/sites/files/jrf/514.pdf

Working with Children

Chapter Outline

Introduction and key questions	163
In what kind of contexts does work with children occur?	164
What rights issues arise for those working with children?	167
What can research tell us about what children want from those who work with them?	172
What positive examples are there of working with children?	175
Summary	182
Further reading	182
Research details	182

Introduction and key questions

While working with children can be an extremely fulfilling occupation, there are also problems and tensions relating to the workplace and children's rights. This chapter considers some of the issues and debates that have been introduced in earlier chapters and considers their particular relevance for those working with children. Activities within the chapter ask you to refer back to previous chapters to support your understanding of the issues that those working with children are faced with. The key questions are as follows:

- In what kind of contexts does work with children occur?
- What rights issues arise for those working with children?
- What can research tell us about what children want from those who work with them?
- What positive examples are there of working with children?

In what kind of contexts does work with children occur?

These are two examples of working with children that illustrate how different the experience of working with children can be.

This example is from Anna Kent, a voluntary worker for Medecin Sans Frontiers in Darfur, a region in the Sudan, where war has affected people's lives for many years (Kent, 2007).

I want to tell you about Nyachoul, a 1-and-a-half year old girl who was brought in two days ago. I was doing the night-shift on-call and got a radio call in my tukul at about 2am that a seriously unwell child had been brought in. As I arrived, it was clear the baby was very ill; she had the remains of a measles rash and she was showing signs of malnourishment and dehydration, which is often a fatal combination. She was dreadfully thin, flopped against her mum like a rag doll, had sunken eye sockets and did not even have the strength to take breast milk. She was silent, as she didn't even have the energy to cry.

I will be honest – I was filled with a variety of emotions. Most were for the well being of the child, but a small amount was directed towards the parents. I thought, 'How could you let your child get this bad before getting help?' There was no time for musing over these thoughts though – we gave the child an NG (a tube from the nose that goes straight into the stomach) and some rehydration liquid, and within a few minutes the baby was alert, looking around and had the strength to start feeding. Over the night we gave her NG nutrients and encouraged her to feed from the mum.

The next day we were able to take out the NG tube and today the baby even started to take some solid therapeutic food, which is great. Her saggy skin has filled out and she has energy to laugh and play (and inevitably cry when the 'kawaii' me – approaches. . . . I am the first white person she has ever seen and I did put an NG tube in her, so I can't really blame her for being afraid of me!)

I have spent some time trying to understand the answer to my initial internal question of the parents . . . how does this happen?? From looking at the parents, they obviously care for the child; they were distraught and they too are very thin. They have explained to me the different pressures their day-to-day lives hold. They live a hard, six-hour walk from the hospital, across swamps and rivers that no doubt hold crocodiles and snakes. Neither of them own shoes and there are no other health services nearer to them. They also had no food from last year's harvest left. They knew they had to cultivate their land to provide food for the rest of the family before the rains started in earnest or they would all go hungry. They realised Nyachuol was sick from the measles, but they felt they couldn't risk the lives of the rest of the family by not digging the sorghum lines.

Compare Anna's experience in a context where people are living with certain kinds of difficulties and where resources are scarce with the following example.

Teresa works in the United Kingdom with children who have special needs. One of the children she works with, Kevin, is 9 years old and cortically blind, is doubly incontinent and epileptic. Here, Teresa is reflecting on a video of her work with Kevin:

> Work with Kevin starts abruptly with me announcing, 'We'll go and find your ball.' . . . When he moves from crouching to a high kneeling position I say, 'good kneeling' but on reflection Kevin's action looked like a communicative gesture of joining in than a mere motor action. Later when the toy organ stops working and I say so Kevin says 'oh dear' . . . again I missed it perhaps because Kevin often says this as a catchphrase. However on this occasion the words were meaningful and deserved a response to underline the fact.
>
> I omit to let Kevin feel the ball at the start of the activity, one of the few ways of working out what is going on. Kevin successfully locates the ball. I reward him with an enthusiastic 'good boy, well done' but did not reinforce the meaning of the situation by saying what he had done.
>
> There is a beautiful snatch of film where Kevin and James interact with each other, a notoriously rare event for children with profound and multiple learning difficulties. To my shame, although I am working with Tim I clearly see this happening and take no affirming action and simply intervene when the contact becomes rough. This effectively terminates the interaction.
>
> The contact begins with Kevin trying to further inflate a silver balloon (the inside of a wine box). Kevin rustles it. James snatches at and rustles it and then Kevin rustles it again and pulls it away. James shrieks and then Kevin pats him on the back, pulling the smaller child towards him. I could intervene sensitively at a number of points . . . Instead I pull the two boys slightly apart with the words 'stop fighting'. On continued replaying of the video it can be seen that after initially pulling James, Kevin says 'be careful' as if telling himself and then becomes gentler an instant before I intervene.
>
> (Lehane 1992 cited in Ghaye and Ghaye, 38–9)

Activity

Anna, working with children (and adults) in Darfur, is mainly concerned with keeping children alive in the very difficult circumstances in which they live and MSF is reliant on voluntary donations for the work it does so she is working with scarce resources. In contrast, Teresa is in a context where the basic requirements for life are taken for granted and her concern is to support a group of children's learning and development through a very sensitive understanding of each individual child.

Each context has challenges but they are very different. Think about the sort of challenges that face Anna and Teresa in relation to issues raised earlier in the book:

a. What kind of rights is Anna likely to be most concerned about? How might these differ from the rights that Teresa might be concerned with? (Chapter 2)
b. Which of the following factors identified in Chapter 6 might be influencing the ability of families to provide for children's rights in each of these contexts?
   - The consumer society
   - Over and under employment
   - Relative poverty
   - The commodification of children as social and emotional assets
   - The perception of danger and blame
   - Absolute poverty
   - Children being economic assets
   - War and political repression

c. Where does the funding for each of these contexts come from? Do these stem from legal or moral considerations? (Chapter 2)
d. What kind of factors might be 'silencing' the voices of the children in each context? (Chapter 4)
e. What might Anna and Teresa be able to do to support the children's voices being heard? (Chapter 4)

Even within one small country like the United Kingdom, the contexts in which professionals work with children are likely to differ, although not as widely as the earlier examples. In the United Kingdom, professionals come from a number of different backgrounds – health, education, care, justice – each bringing their own particular skills but also their own particular emphasis.

Even though the information in Table 7.1 doesn't include those working with children in Health services it is apparent that a large number of people are employed in different ways to support children. Not all services for children are provided by the state: private and voluntary organizations are also concerned with children's education, health, care and leisure and the table shows the large proportion of volunteers that are involved, particularly in the area of sports and recreation. The resulting fragmentation of services for children can lead to difficulties in ensuring that all aspects of a child's life are considered and their rights are met. Every Child Matters (DfES, 2003) is the UK government's response to this challenge and became the backbone of policies relating to children in 2003. The emphasis in the document is on professionals working collaboratively and taking a holistic view of the child. This should mean that, although professionals have a particular specialist focus this would be in

Table 7.1 The range and numbers of adults working with children in England in 2003 (Society Guardian and NCH using info from The Employers' Organization for local government. – Horton, C. (ed.) (2003) *Working with Children* 2004–5, London: Society Guardian)

Service sectors	Paid education, care and support staff	Unpaid staff and volunteers
Education	1,500,000	190,000
Social care	80,000	70,000
Early years	380,000	50,000
Justice and probation	20,000	
Sports, recreation and allied occupations	480,000	1,480,000
Total	2,460,000	1,790,000

the context of understanding the child in relation to their family, peers and community and within these contexts, understanding their individual rights and needs. While ECM is particularly concerned with children who are most vulnerable, for example those in the care system or justice system, it is also concerned with all children and the services that are provided for them through health, education, care and leisure services.

What rights issues arise for those working with children?

The basic tenets of the UNCRC point to the importance of all those who work with or for children being able to understand and support children's rights. As the UNCRC makes clear, while a service may have a particular focus on a particular right or group of rights, their other rights cannot be ignored. For example, the Health service has a child's survival and developmental rights as its key focus, but all those working with children within the service need to ensure children's rights to protection and participation are also given equal consideration. However, this is in the context of children being part of a wider society that also has needs and rights that need to be taken into consideration. In addition, government policies, while ostensibly having children at the heart, are also concerned with the economic and social position of the country. Consequently those who work with children, particularly in services provided by the government, have to work within the framework of their particular service which will have its own priorities. These are reflected in Table 7.2.

Table 7.2 Services for children: key focus and possible tensions

Service sectors	Working with individuals or groups	Key focus	Implications and possible tensions for those working in the service
Health	Individuals	Ensuring children are brought up in circumstances that support health and, when they are ill, providing appropriate health care	Ensuring children's rights to be involved in decisions about their treatment alongside the legal right of parents to make these decisions
Education	Groups	Ensuring children have the knowledge, skills and attitudes that are necessary to be productive and responsible future citizens	Balancing the requirements of society in the form of the curriculum and academic targets for children with children's holistic development and participation Ensuring children are treated as individuals not as a group
Day care and 'wrap around services'	Groups	Ensuring children are cared for, usually while parents are working	Ensuring children are treated as individuals not as a group
Care services	Mainly individuals	Ensuring children who are vulnerable are protected	Balancing protection with children remaining in their family and ensuring children are involved in decision making
Justice	Mainly individuals	Ensuring children conform to the laws of society and dealing with them when they don't	Balancing children's rights with the needs of the wider community
Play and leisure	Groups	Providing opportunities for children to engage in play and leisure activities	Ensuring children are treated as individuals not as a group

---

Activity

1. The services in this table will have norms concerning the space and time that is given to children being involved in decision making. Look back at the Key points Spaces and Norms in Decision making in Chapter 5 (page 115) and see how they fit in with the key focus for each service.
2. The key focus for each service and the implications for those working in the service are likely to reflect different ways of thinking about children and the kinds of relationships that exist between children and adults. Look back at Table 2.4, 'Rights, Children and Adults', in Chapter 2 and think about the kinds of relationship that are implicit in each of the services.

Although all these occupations can be classified as working with children, they also have to work with and take account of the child's parents and family and, in the case of the justice and education system, are very much influenced by the requirements of society for children to conform to certain expectations. The tensions highlighted in earlier chapters involve those that exist

- between ensuring the individual rights of children are met and consideration of the rights and needs of wider society,
- between the rights of the child and the wishes of their parents, and
- between children's rights to participation and protection

are evident across all occupations.

The following are examples of concerns expressed by UK Children's Commissioners' Report (Marshall et al., 2008).

Too many children are being criminalised and brought into the youth justice system at an increasingly young age. Between 2002 and 2006, crime committed by children fell, yet during the same period, it is estimated that there was a 26% increase in the number of children criminalised and prosecuted.

(2008, 34)

We are also concerned about the over-representation of black children in the criminal justice system and evidence of direct or indirect discrimination in policing and the youth justice system.

(2008, 32)

Children are, however, still not viewed as key participants in education: discussions around improving education are often adult-based and fail to include children and their views. We are also concerned that educational inequalities persist, despite considerable investment in education across the UK. Access to sufficient, quality education remains a problem for particular groups (such as Gypsy and Traveller children, children within the juvenile justice system and children in care).

(2008, 27)

Although social services might prefer to be involved in preventative work, family support and early intervention, in reality, financial pressures, demands on staff and an emphasis on the right of the child to be looked after by their parents mean that they often focus on children whose situations have reached crisis point.

(2008, 17)

All these concerns illustrate how national policies affect the context that those who work with children experience and influence the tensions

- between ensuring the individual rights of children are met and consideration of the rights and needs of wider society,
- between the rights of the child and the wishes of their parents, and
- between children's rights to participation and protection.

Activity

Identify the difficulties that workers in these different services might face. Look at the examples in earlier chapters to extend your thinking:

Youth Justice system – research by Kilkelly (page 119–22 in Chapter 5),
Education – the points made by Anderson (page 117) in Chapter 5,
Social Services – the Cleveland enquiry (page 154) in Chapter 6 and Gorin's research
in Chapter 6 (page 156).

In addition to these tensions, there are issues for all those who work with children around gender, class, ethnicity, disability and sexuality. Ensuring that stereotypes are challenged and issues relating to identity are considered are key factors in working with children. This may be particularly difficult for those who work with groups of children, but all workers have a duty to ensure that children's rights are upheld 'without discrimination of any kind, irrespective of the child's or his or her parent's or legal guardian's race, colour, sex, language, religion, political or other opinion, national, ethnic or social origin, property, disability, birth or other status' (UNCRC, 1989 Article 2), but the powerful position that those who work with children have can mean that their own interests and values take precedence over the rights of children.

Example of research: gender inequalities

In reviewing research on children's gendered experiences Morrow (2006) gives and example of how playworkers can ignore children's perceptions of gender differences and create inequalities in their settings:

> Playworkers utilised adult discourses of equality of opportunity when they wanted to prevent what they saw as boys' subversive attempts to take over space, being used by girls, for football. The boys interpreted these adult attempts to limit football in terms of unequal gendered relations in clubs, primarily because most play workers were women. As one 10-year old boy explained: 'They treat girls differently, and they treat boys like they are things that don't belong here'.
>
> (Smith and Barker, 2000, cited in Morrow, 2006, p. 97)

Reflection on research

The workers in this setting were acting in what they believed to be in the best interests of the girls, but this was without getting the perceptions of any of the children. As a result, they were unable to deal with a further tension

- between the rights of individuals or groups of children with particular interests.

Although different professionals will be subject to different kinds of pressures the implications for all workers are that they need to be aware of

- the tensions between the rights of different individuals and groups and develop personal and collective strategies for resolving these,
- the perceptions of all those involved,
- their powerful position in relation to children and to parents/carers.

Activity

How do you think the playworkers might have dealt with the boys' domination of space in a way that left both the boys and the girls feeling that a fair outcome had been reached?

What can research tell us about what children want from those who work with them?

Research into what children would like from those who work with them has largely focused on vulnerable children who have workers who deal with them as individuals. However, the findings may also be relevant to all those who work with children.

Example of research: what children want from those who work with them – 1

The Children Act Now (Aldgate and Statham, 2001) identified qualities in professionals that are important to children:

- reliability – keeping promises;
- practical help;
- the ability to give support;
- time to listen and respond;
- seeing children's lives in the round, not just the problems.

Reflection on research

Activity

Look back at the points that parents made about their relationship with services provided by the state in Chapter 6 (page 155). Identify the similarities in what parents and children are looking for. Why do you think there are some similarities?

Example of research: what children want from those who work with them – 2

Thomas (2000), researching the experience of children in care, identified that what was most important for these children was that their point of view was taken into account and they were taken seriously. At the heart of this was the need for their workers to be good communicators, and they identified a number of factors that were important in ensuring this:

- *Time:* Children want adults to have time to spend with the child and to work at their pace so the child stays in control.
- *Relationships, trust and honesty:* Children want adults who are 'straight' with them.
- *Active listening:* Responding to cues, restating and drawing out the meaning of what the child is saying alongside the expression of warmth, empathy and acceptance.
- *Choice, information and preparation:* Children are more likely to have their say if they have been prepared for the discussion and given time to think.
- *Support and encouragement:* Children don't like 'being put on the spot' and need support to say things that might be difficult. They don't want to be judged or criticized.
- *Activities:* Children identified games, drawing and other activities that can be less boring than sitting and talking.
- *The child's agenda:* Children wanted to be given space to talk about what concerns them.
- *Serious fun:* If decision-making processes are made enjoyable (even around serious topics) children are more likely to get involved.

Reflection on research

Activity
Look back at Chapters 4 and 5 and their concerns with hearing children's voices and participation in decision making. How do you think the features of communication identified by children will support children's voices being heard and their participation in decision making?

Sinclair (2004) argues that this sort of communication can't just be bolted on to ways of working with children but has to be embedded in the kinds of relationships that exist between children and those who work with them. However, it is potentially more difficult for workers in some services to engage in this kind of relationship.

Activity
Think about those such as teachers and day care workers who work with groups of children rather than individuals. Think about those such as teachers and probation officers who are trying to balance the requirements of society with the rights of children.

How easy do you think it is for them to engage in relationships of this kind?

Often the problem lies in the way the service is organized and its underlying beliefs and assumptions. While the organization may believe that it knows what is best for the children it works with, the children themselves may have different ideas.

Example of research: children's response to services

Research by Southon and Dhakal into the lives of Street children in Nepal identified how children used the services provided by voluntary organizations. The intention of most services was to get children off the streets and into mainstream society but the research found that

> Organisations are very much seen as a part of street life and not as a way out. Different organisations are used for different services – food, shelter, medical treatment, emergency support, clothes, shelter, and recreational facilities. It is these open-access services, supporting their independent living, which were positively assessed by children. . . . Street children will continue to use services offered but unless organisations learn to work in the street environment they will have no impact on the important development stage of a significant number of children living on the street.

The following are some of the observations that children made about the different organizations indicating they were very clear about the type of support they needed and their resistance to being controlled by the organizations.

> There is a local group which gives us rice but they always scold us even when eating rice!
>
> (Baneswor, 12 years old)

> Organization D is very good because it sometimes gives food, and gives clothes each year. It gives us medicine and helps us when we are in trouble.
>
> (Baneswor, 13 years old)

> I like organization D very much. They always set a time and come here and wake us up if we are asleep. Other organizations take you to their centre for no reason or scold and bully us. I like organization D because they always keep their promises. They recognize that games and enjoyment are important for us. They stay and eat together with us as brothers. But, there is a long process for training. I don't know when it will be available. I don't have confidence.
>
> (New Bus Park, 15)

> In organization D all the staff love and care for us. This organization is the closest thing to me. Organization A only lets good children stay. They only let small and ill children stay. Organization F have invited me but I haven't been yet.
>
> (Maiti Devi, 14 years old)

Reflection on research

Activity
Organization D appears to be popular with these children. Can you identify some of Thomas' criteria for effective communication in the way that staff from organization D engage with children?

How might Organization D have a different interpretation of 'in the child's best interests' to Organization A?

What positive examples are there of working with children?

So far, this chapter has considered some of the difficulties that those working with children might experience. However, there are many examples of successful working with children of different ages and in different contexts. The two examples that follow provide a focus for thinking about what conditions might contribute to success.

Chapter 5 includes a discussion about the four elements that need to be considered to ensure that a whole-systems approach is established to ensure children's involvement in decision making:

- Culture
- Structure
- Practice
- Review

Look back at this discussion and relate the conditions to the following examples of successful working:

Example of successful working – 1

Case and Haines (2004) report on a project in Swansea that aimed to prevent youth offending in Swansea through a range of initiatives that targeted risk factors. The risk factors were identifies with the aid of the young people and the initiatives were all based on the participation of the young people. The initiatives were as follows:

- *Promoting positive behaviour in schools*. This initiative wasn't just focused on changing the behaviour of the young people in school but was also concerned with tackling the school organization and ethos and developing family–school partnerships.
- *Family Group Conferencing (FGC)*. The restorative justice measure of FGC consists of all appropriate parties involved in school non-attendance or offending behaviour (e.g. young person, family, teachers, friends, victims) meeting to search for a way to find a positive resolution to the situation.
- *Mentoring*. A range of mentoring opportunities was provided, all based on the type of relationship advocated by Thomas (2000).
- *Cognitive-behavioural anger management*. These include individual as well as group sessions and give individuals the opportunity to talk about their perception of their difficulties
- *Youth access*. This acknowledged the difficulties that were experienced by some young people in a school setting and offered alternative settings for education and training to those who were at risk of exclusion.
- *Youth Action Groups (YAG)*. These involve young people in trying to find solutions to some of the risk factors associated with problem behaviours.

The evaluation found that the consultative approach empowered the young people in engaging in positive behaviour and avoiding behaviours that are seen to be anti-social.

Reflections on the research

This kind of work with young people involves both education and justice systems and overcomes some of the tensions around individual rights and the needs of society by involving all interested parties. While it was primarily involved with groups of young people, there were also opportunities through mentoring for young people to engage in individual positive relationships with adults. By involving the young people in identifying risk factors, rather than targeting particular groups on the grounds of socio-economic status or race, the interventions attempted to challenge stereotypes and avoid stigmatizing young people.

Activity
The authors of the research identify that

the key objective is to produce a dynamic cultural shift within the City and County of Swansea such that Promoting Prevention exists as a strategy and a structure, which binds local agencies into a coordinated and comprehensive approach focused on enfranchising the local youth population and targeting disaffection. This requires commitment from all parties if Promoting Prevention is to supersede a more traditional 'signposting' role in order to empower young people's knowledge of and access to services. The ethos and methods of Promoting Prevention seek to create a local climate of change that values the ideals of 'community' and 'citizenship' within an integrated working model.

How do these intentions relate to the four elements: culture, structure, practice and review?

Interview with Kevin Haines and Stephen Case about their research

Stephen Case and Kevin Haines, Centre for Criminal Justice & Criminology, Swansea University

Sue Welch: How do you see the importance of your research in helping those who work with children?

Kevin Haines and Stephen Case: The research and, indeed, Promoting Prevention itself was based on the concept of 'Children First' (first described in Haines and Drakeford, 1998, *Young People and Youth Justice*. Houndmills: Macmillan). Crucially, as we see it, Children First offers practitioners a number of important benefits: it provides a way of focusing on the whole child and not only on the child as offender; it is future oriented – about achieving change in the future rather than focusing on the past (about which little can be done) or past deeds; and it directs work with children onto focusing on positive behaviour and outcomes. Children First does all of this in a manner in which the full engagement of the child is central to the process. Thus, Children First provides a constructive and practical alternative to the punishment of children and the sterile management of risk.

Sue Welch: Did your research prompt any further questions about ways to involve young people and give them a positive view of their place in the community?

Kevin Haines and Stephen Case: The Promoting Prevention research suggests a socially inclusive, empowering, rights-based and participatory approach to perceptions of and work with children and young people. The methodology employed attempted to reorientate the more traditional deficit- and risk-based focus of research and practice by advocating for the potential of universalized methods of consultation and the promotion of positive behaviour as means of achieving both prosocial behaviour and reductions in risk and negative outcomes. Of particular importance was the utility of multiple agencies working together as a 'team around the child' to address needs expressed by the child (as opposed to risks perceived by an adult) through multiple, responsive interventions that were both targeted and universal, but always delivered in an inclusive and non-stigmatizing fashion. Central to both Promoting Prevention itself and to the research was the constructive and positive involvement of children in setting priorities and engagement in delivering outcomes.

This project involved children aged 11–18 so it might be thought that it is only possible to engage with children in these ways when they are older. However, a lot of work has been taking place with very young children to find ways of listening to and taking account of their thoughts and feelings in the settings that they attend. This has been particularly effective in Day Care and Early Years settings.

Example of successful working – 2

Research by Alison Clark (2001) with children aged 6 months to 5 years of age used a range of techniques (a 'mosaic' approach) to gain children's views about their setting. The techniques included

- Observations
- Interviewing and child conferencing
- Cameras
- Tours with the children guiding the adult
- Map making
- Parent and practitioner views.

Information from all these sources was brought together in order to understand what children were concerned about. They found that

- friends and changing friendships, including relationships with important adults and siblings;
- favourite spaces including 'hidden' spaces outside;
- conflict and how it is dealt with by adults;
- memories of important people who have left and aspirations about the future

were all important to the children and this helped those working with them to adapt the environment and the way they worked to take account of these concerns.

Again, this example involves children as well as parents and professionals in decision making and gives opportunities for children to engage with adults individually in ways that are appropriate to their means of communication. It also ensures inclusion through the variety of communication techniques used.

Activity
Look back at the Ask Us! Example in Chapter 4 (pages 99–100). Identify the common factors in the mosaic approach and Ask us! example.

⇨

While these examples illustrate the positive aspects of listening to children and young people in order to improve their lives Moss (2006) urges caution that adults working in this way need to be sure that

- they are aware of the unequal power relationships that might exist so, even in the Early Years setting some children might be more vocal than others and their voice may take priority;
- 'listening to children' can be tokenistic unless there is a willingness to act on what is heard;
- even more dangerously, by asking children about what they think and feel, there is the potential to use this information in ways that don't have benefits for the children: a means of manipulating children.

Activity

These pointers echo points that are made in Chapter 4 Table 4.2 (page 89) on 'Silence and Voice', and 'Key Ideas: Voice and Participation Rights', (page 90), concerning children's voices and participation in decision making. Look back at these chapters and identify what the implications are for those working with children.

Activities

The following activities are designed to help reflect back over the book as a whole. Key themes are identified with activities that relate to the theme in a number of chapters.

Theme 1 – the children's rights agenda: silencing and voice

Chapter 4 identified three particular ways that can be helpful in considering the complex factors silencing children when working with children. These were as follows:

- The worth of children's voices,
- The ways that social exclusion silences children,
- The dominance of adult orientated ways of communicating and decision making.

The following activities ask you to review the research examples in relation to these three kinds of factor.

a. The first factor was described as

a child's voice is not given *worth,* in terms of adults not treating their ideas or opinions as having value or legitimacy. Here the idea of 'voice' is attached to areas such as judgement, maturity, capability and power.

Review the ways of working with children, as described in Chapter 5 (page 123), and drawn from Weijers (2004), and identify how the right to participate was engaged with positively in terms of ideas of worth, judgement, maturity, capability and power.

b. The second was described as

'broad factors that exclude sectors of the population have an impact upon the children's participation' including poverty, class, gender, disability and sexuality.

Review the ways of working with children described in Chapter 4, 'Example of Research: Ask Us!', and identify how the right to participate was engaged with in ways that relate to challenging factors relating to the exclusion experienced by children in relation to society's attitudes towards disability.

c. The third was described as

barriers to children's right to participate . . . adult-orientated ways of communication and involvement in participation.

Review the ways of working with children described in Chapter 7, 'Example of Successful Working 2', and identify how the right to participate was engaged with in ways that developed ways of communicating and participating that were child centred and addressed barriers set up by adult ways of communication and involvement.

Theme 2 – rights-informed approaches to relating to children: decision making

Chapter 5 discussed the Social Care Institute for Excellence's guide to enabling the participation of children and young people in work concerning social care. They proposed that even when an organization says that it is committed to a culture of participation, they do not always change their ways of working as a result. Their argument includes the idea that unless children and young people can influence decision-making processes their right to participate will not be effectively realized. They proposed four areas to assist in organizations review. Chapter 5 summarized the elements that combine to enable decision making:

Culture: the ethos of an organization, shared by all staff and service users, which demonstrates a commitment to participation;

Structure: the planning, development and resourcing of participation evident in an organization's infrastructures;

Practice: the ways of working, methods for involvement, skills and knowledge which enable children and young people to become involved;

Review: the monitoring and evaluation systems which enable an organization to evidence change affected by children and young people's participation.

Re-examine the two following examples of research into practice with children: 'Example of Research: Rights, Families and Religion', Chapter 6 (pages 147–8), and 'Example of Research: Consultation with Young Children', Chapter 4 (pages 104–5).

a. Does the example indicate whether the culture demonstrates a commitment to *participation*? If it does – how does it do that? If not, how do you think change could be effected to create such a culture? In reflecting on this think especially about the organizational *structures* that are in place, or that could be changed.

b. Does the example include effective *practice* – ways of working or methods – that enables children and young people to be involved? If it does – how does it do that? If not, how do you think change could be effected to create methods? In reflecting on this think especially about whether there is effective involvement of children in *reviewing* the organization.

Theme 3 – tensions, spaces and relationships: family, best interest and rights

Chapter 1 discussed the idea that an emerging theme within children's rights concerned tensions 'between the different spaces and relationships within which children live their lives. One of this book's key themes concerns the tensions between children's experiences of spaces where rights informed policies and laws operate and where they do not.' Chapter 6 discussed a key aspect of this tension, concerning the relationship between children's rights, children's position in their family and issues concerning those working with children. It talks about the relationship between the concept of 'best interests' and the role of carer in the following way:

> the concept of 'the child's best interests' makes it clear that carers need to be aware of the power relationship that they have with the child and acknowledge that their personal interests may be in conflict with the child's. Knowing the child's thoughts on the matter can only be beneficial in trying to make the best decision.

> The main implication of these ideas is that in order for carers to act in the best interests of the child, they need to be aware of and respect the views of the child. This doesn't mean that the child will always do exactly what he or she wants but he or she will participate in discussions about what actions might be best. Interestingly, Thomas's research into children's participation in decision making found that 'what they wanted was above all the opportunity to take part in dialogue with adults, not for either themselves or the adults to determine the outcome' (146).

Look back at the examples.

Decision Making and Participation Rights in Education, Chapter 5
Example of Research: Participation and Protection, Chapter 6,
Example of Research: Children's Response to Services, Chapter 7
What ideas about 'the best interests of the child' emerge from the adults and children in the examples?
How are children's views of what they think is in their 'best interests' taken into account?
How might the dialogue between adults and children concerning what is 'in the child's best interests' be supported in each example?

⇨

Summary

This chapter has

- explored the contexts of working with children and the different challenges that are posed,
- identified the rights issues that arise for those working with children,
- considered how social policy influences those issues through the demands made on workers,
- discussed how research can inform us about children's views of those who work with them,
- given two positive examples of working with children in ways that encourage their participation through positive relationships.

Further reading

Thomas N. (2000) *Children, Family and the State: Decision-Making and Child Participation*. London: Macmillan.

Chapter 6, 'Children Looked after by the State', considers the experiences of looked after children and the implications for those who work with them.

Walker, G. (2008) *Working Together for Children: A Critical Introduction to Multi-agency Working*. London: Continuum.

This book considers the theoretical and practical implications of children's rights for those working with children and the different perspectives of different professionals.

Research details

Example of research: gender inequalities

This review of UK research looks at children's accounts of their daily lives and the gender differences in these accounts.

Morrow, V. (2006) 'Understanding gender differences in context', *Children & Society*, 20(2), 92–100.

Example of research: what children want from those who work with them – 1

Following the introduction of the Children Act 24 research studies were commissioned to look at the effectiveness of implementation. This report gives details of the individual studies and draws out the main findings on important issues across the studies.

Aldgate, J. and Statham, J. (2001) *The Children Act Now: Messages from Research*. Norwich: HMSO.

Example of research: what children want from those who work with them – 2

The research undertaken by Thomas was intended to find out how far children in local authority care were involved in decision making and it is reported as chapters in a book. The research was carried out in seven local authorities and took the form of a quantitative survey of children and a series of open-ended interviews with children, social workers, carers and parents.

Thomas, N. (2000). *Children, Family and the State: Decision-making and Child Participation*. London: Macmillan.

Example of research: children's response to services

This research, into the lives of street children in Nepal was funded by Save the Children. It was carried out by trained researchers from the street children who undertook individual interviews and focus group discussions with other children.

Southon, J. and Dhakal, P. (2003) 'A life without basic service: Street children say', *Save the Children*. Available online at www.savethechildren.net/nepal/key_work/street_children.html

Example of successful working – 1

The Promoting Prevention initiative to prevent youth offending in Swansea was evaluated with a computer-based interactive questionnaire with 580 young people aged between 11 and 18 years.

Case, S. and Haines, K. (2004) 'Promoting prevention: Evaluating a multi-agency initiative of youth consultation and crime prevention in Swansea', *Children & Society*, 18, 355–70.

Example of successful working – 2

This report by the Thomas Coram Early Childhood Centre describes and evaluates the usefulness of techniques that have been used to help adults understand the views of very young children.

Clark, A. and Moss, P. (2001) *Listening to Young Children: The Mosaic Approach*. London: NCB Enterprises.

References

Ahmad, S. Akbar, A. Akbar, H. Ayub, S. Batool, A. Batool, S., Hussain, B. Kiani, S. Mahmood, S. and Rauf, R.(2008) 'East meets West – why do some South Asian young people feel they need to lead a double identity and how does cultural and religious issues affect them?' *Young Researchers Network.* Available online at http://childrens-research-centre.open.ac.uk/research/Barnardo'sresearchreport.pdf

Alanen, L. and Mayall, B. (2001) *Conceptualizing Child-adult Relations.* London: Routledge/Falmer.

Alderson, P. (2008) *Young Children's Rights Exploring Beliefs, Principles and Practice.* London: Jessica Kingsley Publications.

Alderson, P. and Montgomery, J. (1996a) *Health Care Choices Making Decisions with Children.* London: Institute for Public Policy Research.

Alderson, P. and Montgomery, J. (1996b) 'What about me?' *Health Service Journal,* 11, 22–4.

Aldgate, J. and Statham, J. (2001) *The Children Act Now: Messages from Research.* Norwich: HMSO.

Alston, P. and Tobin, J. (2005) *Laying the Foundations for Children's Rights.* Florence: UNICEF, Innocenti Research Centre.

Anderson, K. (2008) 'Sidelined: The marginalisation of children's voices in education', *Child Right, Journal of Law & Policy Affecting Children & Young People,* October, 18–21.

Archard, D. (1993) *Children: Rights and Childhood.* London: Routledge.

Archard, D. and Macleod, C. (2002) *The Moral and Political Status of Children.* Oxford: Oxford University Press.

Arneil, B. (2002) 'Becoming versus being: A critical analysis of the child in liberal theory', in Archard, D. and Macleod, C. (eds) *The Moral and Political Status of Children.* Oxford: Oxford University Press.

Ask Us! (2003) *Children's Society Report.* Available online at http://sites.childrenssociety.org.uk

Australian National Childcare Accreditation Council. (2007) *Young children and decision makers.* Available online at www.ncac.gov.au/factsheets/factsheet2

Bach, M. (2002) 'Social inclusion as solidarity: Rethinking the child rights agenda', *Perspectives on Social Inclusion Working Paper Series.* Toronto: The Laidlaw Foundation.

Badham, B. (2004) 'Participation for a change; Disabled young people lead the way', *Children & Society,* 18, 143–54.

Barton, L. (2003) *Inclusive Education and Teacher Education: A Basis for Hope or a Discourse of delusion?* London: Institute of Education, University of London

BBC News. Available online at news.bbc.co.uk/1/hi/uk ch 3

Irish Refugee Council. Available online at www.irishrefugeecouncil.ie/press06/separated_children.html

Bell, B., Brett, R., Marcus, R. and Muscroft, S. (1999) *Children's Rights: Reality or Rhetoric? The UN Convention on the Rights of the Child: The First Ten Years.* London: Save the Children.

Bisin, S. (2007) *New School Sanitation Brings Positive Behaviours.* Islamabad, Pakistan: UNICEF Pakistan – Real Lives. Available online at www.unicef.org/pakistan/reallives_3882.htm

Boyden, J. and De Berry, J. (2004) *Children and Youth on the Front Line: Ethnography, Armed Conflict, and Displacement.* Oxford: Berghan.

Brannen, J. and O'Brien, M. (1996) *Children in Families: Research and Policy.* London: Falmer Press.

Brighouse, H. (2002) 'What rights (if any) do children have?' in Archard, D. and Macleod, C. (eds) *The Moral and Political Status of Children.* Oxford: Oxford University Press.

Broadhead, P., Meleady, C. and Delgado, M. A. (2008) *Children, Families and Communities.* Maidenhead: Open University Press.

Burchardt, T. (2008) 'Time and income poverty', *CASE Report 57.* London: London School of Economics. Available online at http://sticerd.lse.ac.uk/dps/case/cr/CASEreport57.pdf

Case, S. and Haines, K. (2004) 'Promoting prevention: Evaluating a multi-agency initiative of youth consultation and crime prevention in Swansea', *Children & Society*, 18, 355–70.

Children's Rights Agenda. Available online at www.projects.tigweb.org/cranigeria

Clark, A. and Moss P. (2001) *Listening to Young Children: The Mosaic Approach.* London: NCB enterprises.

Cohen, B., Moss, P., Petrie, P. and Wallace, J. (2004) *A New Deal for Children? Re-forming Education and care in England, Scotland and Sweden.* Bristol: Policy Press.

Combe, V. (2002) *Up for It: Getting Young People Involved in Local Government.* London: The National Youth Agency.

Children's Rights Alliance for England. (2000) *The REAL Democratic Deficit: Why 16- and 17-year-olds Should Be Allowed to Vote.* London: CRAE Publications.

Children's Rights Alliance of England. (2008a) *Survey Children's Rights.* London CRAE Publications.

Children's Rights Alliance. (2008b) *Convention on the Rights of the Child.* Available online at www.crae.org.uk/rights/uncrc.html

Children's Rights Alliance (2008c) *Human Rights Act.* Available online at www.crae.org.uk/rights/hra.html

Children's Society. (2009) *The Good Childhood Enquiry: What Children Told Us.* Available online at www.childrenssociety.org.uk/resources/documents/good%20childhood/14690_full.pdf

Council of Europe. (1950) *The European Convention on Human Rights.* Available online at www.hri.org/docs/ECHR50.html

Dalrymple, J. (2005) 'Constructions of child and youth advocacy: Emerging issues in advocacy practice', *Children & Society*, 19(1), 3–15.

Davey, C. (2008) *What Do They Know? Investigating the Human Rights Concerns of Children and Young People Living in England.* London: Children's Rights Alliance for England.

Department for Children, Schools and Families. (2003) *Every Child Matters.* Available online at everychildmatters.gov.uk

Department for Children, Schools and Families. (2003) School Admissions Code of Practice. Available online at www.dcsf.gov.uk/sacode

Department for Children, Schools and Families/ Children's Rights Alliance. (2007) *Ready Steady Change.* London: Department for Children, Schools and Families/CRAE.

Department for Education and Skills. (2004) *Every Child Matters: Change for Children.* London: Department for Education and Skills.

Department of Health. (1989) *Children Act.* Available online at www.dh.gov.uk/en/ Publicationsandstatistics

Department of Health. (2001) *Seeking Consent: Working with Child*ren. London: Department of Health.

Department of Health. (2002) *Listening, Hearing and Responding: Core Principles for the Involvement of Children and Young People.* London: Department of Health.

Directgov: Public Services All in One Place. Available online at http://www.direct.gov.uk/en/Parents/ ParentsRights/DG_4002954

Dowty, T. (2008) 'Pixie-dust and Privacy: What's Happening to Children's Rights in England?' *Children & Society,* 22, 393–9.

Engle, P. (2006) *Comparative Policy Implications of Children's Rights in United Nations Committee on the Rights of the Child, United Nations' Children's Fund and 'Implementing Child Rights in Early Childhood' : A Guide to General Comment 7'. Implementing Child Rights in Early Childhood.* The Hague: Bernard van leer Foundation.

Etzioni, A. (1995) *The Spirit of Community: Rights, Responsibilities and the Communitarian Agenda.* London: Fontana.

European Union. (2006a) *Strategy on the Rights of a Child.* Available online at http://ec.europa.eu/ justice

European Union. (2006b) *You and the EU! The European Commission's Children's Rights Policy.* Available online at www.crin.org/docs/FileManager/euronet/childfriendlyversion1317yrs.pdf

Flewitt, R. (2005) 'Is every child's voice heard?: Researching the different ways 3-year-old children communicate and make meaning at home and in a preschool playgroup', *Early Years: An International Journal of Research and Development,* 25(3), 207–22.

Franklin, B. (2002) *The New Handbook of Children's Rights: Comparative Policy and Practice.* London: Routledge.

Franklin, A. and Sloper, P. (2005) 'Listening and responding? Children's participation in health care within England', *International Journal of Children's Rights,* 13(1/2), 11–29.

Franklin, A. and Sloper, P. (2006) 'Participation of disabled children and young people in decision making within social services departments: A survey of current and recent activities in England', *British Journal of Social Work,* 36(5), 723–41.

Freeman, M. (2000) 'The Future of Children's Rights', *Children & Society, 14,* 277–93.

Ghaye, A. and Ghaye, K. (1998) *Teaching and Learning through Critical Reflective Practice.* London: David Fulton.

Gorin, S. (2004) *Understanding What Children Say: Children's Experiences of Domestic Violence, Parental Substance Misuse and Parental Health Problems.* York: Joseph Rowntree Foundation/The National Children's Bureau.

Haines, K. and Drakeford, M. (1998) *Young People and Youth Justice.* Houndmills: Macmillan.

Griggs, J. and Walker, R. (2008) *The Costs of Child Poverty for Individuals and Society: A Literature Review.* York: Joseph Rowntree Foundation.

Henricson, C. and Bainham, A. (2005) *The Child and Family Policy Divide*. York: Joseph Rowntree Foundation.

Her Majesty's Inspectorate of Prisons. (2008) *Report on an Announced Inspection of Yarl's Wood Immigration Removal Centre*. London: Crown Publications.

Hill, M. and Tisdall, K. (1997) *Children and Society*. London and New York: Longman.

Horton, C. (ed.) (2003) *Working with Children* 2004–5, London: Society Guardian.

Horwath, J., Lees, J., Sidebotham, P., Higgins, J. and Imitiaz, A. (2008) *Religion, Beliefs and Parenting Practices*. York: Joseph Rowntree Foundation.

Ignatieff, M. (2003) *Human Rights as Politics and Idolatry*. Princeton, NJ: Princeton University Press.

James, A. and McNamee, S. (2004) 'Can children's voices be heard in family proceedings? Family Law and the construction of childhood in England and Wales', *Representing Children*, 16(3), 168–78.

Jebb, E. (1923) *Declaration on the Rights of the Child*. London: International Save the Children Alliance. Available online at www.crin.org/resources/infoDetail.asp?ID=1306

Jensen, A. (2003) 'For the children's sake', in Jensen, A. and McKee, L. (eds) *Children and the Changing Family*. London: Routledge/Falmer.

Jones, P. (2009) *Rethinking Childhood*. London: Continuum.

Kent, A. (2007) *Impossible Choices, MSF Letters from Sudan*. Available online at www.msf.org.uk/letterwriter.aspx?fId=annakent&lId=c30321ca-5eaf-4f6f-866d-0253fa2cde95

Kilkelly, U., Kilpatrick, R., Lundy, L., Moore, L., Scraton, P., Davey, C., Dwyer, C. and McAlister, A. (2005) *Children's Rights in Northern Ireland*. Belfast: NICCY and Queens' University of Belfast.

Kilkelly, U. (2008) 'Youth courts and children's rights: The Irish experience', *Youth Justice*, 8(110), 39–56.

Laming, W. (2003) *The Victoria Climbié Inquiry: Summary Report of an Inquiry by Lord Laming*. Available online at www.victoria-climbie-inquiry.org.uk

Lansdowne, R. (1996) *Children in Hospital: A Guide for Family and Carers*. Oxford: Oxford University Press.

Leonard, M. (2004) 'Children's views on children's right to work: Reflections from Belfast', *Childhood*, 11, 45–61.

Lewis, A. (2009) 'Silence in the context of "child voice"', *Children & Society*, 24(1), 14–23.

Liebel, M. (2007) 'The New International Labour Organization (ILO) Report on Child Labour – A success story, or the ILO still at a loss?' *Childhood*, 14(2), 279–84.

Lowden, J. (2002) 'Children's rights: A decade of dispute', *Journal of Advanced Nursing*, 37(1), 100–7.

MacNaughton, G., Hughes, P. and Smith, K. (2007) 'Young children's rights and public policy: Practices and possibilities for citizenship in the early years', *Children & Society*, 21, 458–69.

MacNaughton, G., Smith, K. and Lawrence, H. (2003) *ACT Children's Strategy – Consulting with Children Birth to Eight Years of Age. Hearing Young Children's Voices*. London: Children's Services Branch, ACT Department of Education, Youth and Family Services.

Madge, N. (2006) *Children These Days*. Bristol: Policy Press.

Marlowe, J. (1996) 'Helpers, helplessness and self-help', in Gopfert, M. Webster, J. and Seeman, M. (eds) *Parental Psychiatric Disorder, Distressed Parents and Their Families*. Cambridge: Cambridge University Press.

Marshall, K., Lewsley, P., Towler, K. and Aynsley-Green, A. (2008) *UK Children's Commissioners' Report to the UN Committee on the Rights of the Child*. London: 11 Million/NICCY/SCCYP/Children's Commissioner for Wales.

Mason, J. and Falloon, J. (2001) 'Some Sydney children define abuse: Implications for agency in childhood', in Alanen, L. and Mayall, B. (eds) *Conceptualizing Child-Adult Relations*. London: Routledge/Falmer.

McCall, D. S. (2009) *Selected Case Studies of Youth Involvement in Public Decision-Making*. Centre on Community and School Health, Canadian Association for School Health for the Children and Youth Division. Available online at www.schoolfile.com/cash/youthinvolvement.htm

Mill, J. S. (1859) *On Liberty*. London: Parker and Son.

Moorehead, C. (1997) 'Despite safeguards, children's rights are still ignored'. *Press Release*, 26 March 1997. Available online at http://pangaea.org/street_children/world/unconv3.htm

Morris, A. (2004) 'Youth justice in New Zealand', *Crime and Justice*, 31, 243.

Morrow, V. (2006) 'Understanding gender differences in context', *Children & Society*, 20(2), 92–104.

Moss, P. (2002) 'From children's services to children's spaces'. Paper presented at Seminar 1 of the *ESRC Seminar Series: Challenging 'Social Inclusion'. Perspectives for and from Children and Young People*, University of Edinburgh.

Moss, P (2006) 'Listening to young children – beyond rights to ethics', in *Perspectives: A Series of Occasional Papers on Early Years Education: Let's Talk about Listening to Children: Towards a Shared Understanding for Early Years Education in Scotland*. Scotland: Learning and Teaching Scotland.

Cohen, B., Moss, P., Petrie, P. and Wallace, J. (2004) *A new deal for children? Re-forming education and care in England, Scotland and Sweden*. London: Policy Press.

National Youth Agency. (2005) *Involving Children and Young People – An Introduction*. London: National Youth Agency. Available online at www.nya.org.uk

O'Keeffe, A. (2008) 'Their right to liberty', *New Statesman*. Available online at www.newstatesman.com/uk-politics/2008/12immigration-detention-children

O'Neill, O. (1984) 'Paternalism and partial autonomy', *Journal of Medical Ethics*, 10, 173–8.

Olsen, F. (1992) 'Children's rights: Some feminist approaches to the United Nations Convention on the Rights of the Child', *International Journal of Law and the Family*, 6, 192–220.

Osler, A. and Osler, C. (2002) 'Inclusion, exclusion and children's rights: A case study of a student with Asperger syndrome', *Emotional and Behavioural Difficulties*, 7(1), 35–54.

Pain, R. (2000) *Introducing Social Geographies*. London: Arnold.

Parental Rights. (2008) *Protecting Children by Empowering Parents*. Available online at www.parentalrights.org/learn/the-attack-on-parental-rights/international-law.

Penn, H. (2001) 'Culture and childhood in pastoralist communities: The example of outer Mongolia', in Alanen, L. and Mayall, B. (eds) *Conceptualizing Child-Adult Relations*. London: Routledge/Falmer.

Prout, A. (2000) 'Children's participation: Control and self-realisation in British Late Modernity', *Children & Society*, 14, 304–15.

Punch, S. (2001) 'Negotiating autonomy: Childhoods in rural Bolivia', in Alanen, L. and Mayall, B. (eds) *Conceptualising Child-Adult Relations*. London: Routledge/Falmer.

Qvortrup J., Bardy M., Sgritta G. and Wintersberg, H. (1994) *Childhood Matters*. Aldershot: Avebury.

Reading, R., Bissell, S., Goldhagen, J., Harwin, J., Masson, J., Moynihan, S., Parton, N., Pais, M., Thoburn, J. and Webb, E. (2008) 'Promotion of children's rights and prevention of child maltreatment', *The Lancet*, 10, 1016.

Redmond, G. (2008) 'Child poverty and child rights: Edging towards a definition', *Journal of Children and Poverty*, 14(1), 63–82.

Rivers, I. and Cowie, H. A. (2006) 'Bullying and homophobia in UK schools: A perspective on factors affecting resilience and recovery', *Journal of Gay and Lesbian Issues in Education*, 3(4), 11–43.

Sandbaek, M. and Hafdis Einarsson, J. (2008) 'Children and young people report to the UN on their rights'. *NOVA Report*, 2b/08. Available online at www.reassess.no/index

Save the Children. (2006) *From Camp to Community: Liberia Study on Exploitation of Children*. Available online at www.savethechildren.org/publications/liberia-exploitation

Save the Children. (2007) *The Small Hand of Slavery*. London: Save the Children. Available online at www.savethechildren.org.uk/en/docs/child_slavery_briefing.pdf

Save the Children. (2007) *You Could Always Begin by Listening to Us: A Consultation with Children on the EC Communication 'Towards an EU Strategy on the Rights of the Child'*. Available online at www.crin. org/ . . . /You_could_always_begin_by_listening_to_us_SC_Child_ Consultation%202007.pdf

Save the Children. (2008) *Personal Stories Thirteen and Homeless in Nairobi*. London: Save the Children. Available online at www.savethechildren.org.uk/en/55_4203.htm

Sinclair, R. (2004) 'Participation in practice: Making it meaningful, effective and sustainable', *Children & Society*, 18, 106–118.

Sligo, J. (2003). 'Young people's participation in local government initiatives: Rural and urban case studies', *Research Summary Report*. New Zealand: Children's Issues Centre, University of Otago.

Social Care Institute for Excellence. (2006) *SCIE Guide 11: Involving Children and Young People in Developing Social Care*. Available online at www.scie.org.uk/publications/guides/guide11/index.asp

Southon, J. and Dhakal, P. (2003) *A Life without Basic Service: Street Children Say, Save the Children*. Available online at www.savethechildren.net/nepal/key_work/street_children.html

Stafford, A., Laybourne, A. and Hill, M. (2003) '"Having a say": Children and young people talk about consultation', *Children & Society*, 17, 361–73.

Stuart, M. and Baines, C. (2004) *Safeguards for Vulnerable Children*. London: Joseph Rowntree Foundation.

Thomas N. (2000) *Children, Family and the State: Decision-making and Child Participation*. London: Macmillan.

Tomasevski, K. (2004) *Manual on Rights Based Education*. Bangkok: UNESCO.

Tomlinson, P. (2008) 'The politics of childhood', in Jones, P., Moss, D., Tomlinson, P. and Welch, S. (eds) *Childhood: Services and Provision for Children*. London: Pearson.

UNESCO. (2008) *Working Document: Inclusive Education Public Policy*. Geneva: Conference Publication, UNESCO.

UNICEF. (1989). *Summary of the UNCRC Made for Children*. Available online, www.unicef.org.uk

UNICEF. (2006) *Join It All Up: Every Child Matters, The Five Outcomes and the UN Convention on the Rights of the Child*. Available online www.everychildmatters.gov.uk/_files/F1B3FBF728B196018-E9616C71D0BF592.pdf

United Nations. (1948) *Universal Declaration of Human Rights*. Available online at www.un.org/Overview/rights.html

United Nations. (1989) *Convention on the Rights of the Child, Geneva*. Washington, DC: Office of the United Nations High Commissioner for Human Rights. Available online at www.unhchr.ch/html/menu3/b/k2crc.htm

United Nations Committee on Rights of the Child. (2002) *Concluding Observations: UK of Great Britain and Northern Ireland*. Available online at www.unhcr.org/refworld

United Nations Committee on Rights of the Child. (2003) *General Comments No, 5: General Measures of Implementation of the Convention. On the Rights of the Child* (parts 4, 42 and 44). Available online at www.unhcr.org/refworld

United Nations Committee on the Rights of the Child. (2008) *General Comment No 1: The Aims of Education*. Available online at www.unhcr.org/refworld

United Nations Office for the Coordination of Humanitarian Affairs Integrated Regional Information Networks. (2002) *West Africa: Putting Children's Rights on the Military Agenda*. Available online at www.irinnews.org

Wade, A. and Smart, C. (2003) 'As fair as it can be?: Childhood after divorce', in Jensen, A. and McKee, L. (eds) *Children and the Changing Family*. London: Routledge/Falmer.

Waldfogel, J. and Garnham, A. (2008) *Childcare and Child Poverty*. York: Joseph Rowntree Foundation. Available online at www.jrf.org.uk/sites/files/jrf/2267-poverty-children-childcare.pdf

Walker, G. (2008) *Working Together for Children: A Critical Introduction to Multi-agency Working*. London: Continuum.

Weijers, I. (2002) 'Restoration and the family: A pedagogical point of view', in L. Walgrave (ed.) *Restorative Justice and the Law* (pp. 68–81). Cullompton: Willan Publishing.

Weijers, I. (2004) 'Requirements for communication in the courtroom: A comparative perspective on the Youth Court in England/Wales and The Netherlands', *Youth Justice: The Journal of the National Association for Youth Justice*, 4(1), 22–31.

White, S. (2007) 'Children's rights and the imagination of community in Bangladesh', *Childhood*, 14, 505–20.

Willis, C. (1998) *Decision Making, the Foundation for Responsible Behaviour, Working with the Young Child: Ages 4–8*. Arizona: University Of Arizona Bulletins.

Willow C. (2002) *Participation in Practice: Children and Young People as Partners in Change*. London: Save the Children.

Wise, K. (2004) 'Wand-waver lacks magic', *Community Care*, June, 36–7. Available online at www.communitycare.co.uk/Articles/2004/06/03/44989/wand-waver-lacks-magic.html

Youth on Board. (1999) *14 Points: Successfully Involving Youth in Decision Making*. Somerville, MA: Youth on Board. Available online at www.youthonboard.org

Index

abuse 17, 35, 53, 54, 56, 72, 98, 152–4, 162, 164, 170, 198
adults 5, 21, 29, 30, 35, 57, 58, 60, 107, 117, 125, 127, 132, 136, 156, 170, 190
advocacy 20, 96, 107
age 10, 15, 17, 32–4, 37, 42, 43, 44, 53
agency 66, 143, 145, 155, 160
Ask Us! 99–106
asperger's syndrome 6
asylum 33, 79, 80, 82, 105, 144
Australia 25, 87, 143

Bangladesh 34, 35, 56
'best interests' 23, 44, 47, 51, 52, 57, 66, 69, 70, 76, 89, 135, 145, 146, 152, 156, 159, 181
Bill of Rights 31
Border Agency 69
bullying 141, 174, 189

Canadian Association for School Health (CASH) 127, 133, 188
CCTV 78
Charter on the Rights and Welfare of the African Child 63
Charter on the Rights of the Child 40
child centred philosophy 5
child labour 6, 144, 160
child migrants 23, 69
Child Rights Agenda (CRA) 16, 18
Children Act 75, 98, 120
Children First 133, 177
Children's Commissioner 64, 71, 72, 156
Children's Rights Alliance for England (CRAE) 7, 14, 23, 42, 53, 69
citizenship 104, 177

community 5, 8, 34–5, 39, 40, 50, 53, 56, 65, 68, 105, 110, 141, 148, 157, 178
competency 28, 96–7
Connexions 112
culture 37, 44, 48, 56, 129–31, 147, 149, 150–1, 152, 175, 177, 180

decision making 8, 17, 18–19, 20, 25, 46, 61, 74–5, 87, 88, 110–33, 173, 175, 180–1, 183
democracy 38–9, 105, 114
Department for Children, Schools and Families 30
and Ready Steady Change 20
Department for Education and Science 127
Department of Health 75, 93, 97
disability 20, 64, 75, 88, 98, 99, 109, 140, 170–1, 180
discourse and rights 30, 34–5, 37, 144
discrimination 11, 17, 31, 40, 43, 45, 47, 54, 65, 78, 95, 98, 140, 169
duty 34–7, 63, 97, 138, 147

Economic Community of West African States 17
economics 54, 161
education 39, 41, 44, 64, 68, 70, 73, 89, 90, 93, 100, 105, 109, 114–16, 167–9, 170, 176
and inclusive education 64, 98
equality 14, 38, 67–8, 98, 133, 171
emotional and behavioural difficulties 6, 122, 155
equality 24, 48, 67, 68, 107, 133, 171
ethnography 16

European Commission Children's Rights Policy 9
European Union Strategy on the Rights of A Child 7, 9, 10
Every Child Matters 26, 49, 72, 166
exclusion 6, 11, 18, 64, 78, 87, 91, 95, 97, 99, 100, 113, 118, 141, 176, 179, 180
exploitation 44, 46, 62, 77, 144–5, 158

family 8, 9, 25, 32, 35, 39, 41, 50, 62–3, 71, 91, 93, 105, 112, 122, 135–60, 164, 170, 176
food 36, 71, 140, 144, 154, 164, 174

gay 73, 88
gender 20, 35, 88, 95, 98, 104, 140, 170, 180, 182
government (national) 9, 11, 16, 21, 25, 32–3, 66, 69, 72, 86, 110, 117, 135, 167 (local) 19, 54, 87, 112, 127

health 25, 32, 33, 39, 44, 66, 70, 75, 77, 93, 97, 121, 123, 153, 166–8
HM Inspectorate of Prisons 23, 69, 70
hospitals 85, 91, 115, 131, 164
Human Rights Act (1998) 42, 66, 86

immigration 69, 70, 71–2
inclusion 6, 18, 49, 63, 64, 98, 99, 103, 178
inclusive education 64, 98
income 33, 70, 139, 141, 153, 161
inequality 16, 70
information technology 78
Ireland 119–25
Irish Refugee Council 95

Joseph Rowntree Foundation 98, 99, 109, 156, 160–1

language 15, 16, 35, 41, 45, 88, 98, 99, 121–2, 171
law 21, 24, 36, 42, 47, 66–7, 75, 85, 87, 111, 115, 119–25, 137, 152, 157
legislation 8, 13, 26, 42, 52, 54, 64, 68, 75, 89, 102, 118, 135
leisure 14, 32, 38, 41, 44, 64, 70, 100, 114, 139, 140, 142, 166, 167–8

lesbian 73, 88
Liberia 6

market economy 39
maturity 23, 43, 46, 47, 51, 88, 97, 111, 120, 122, 159, 179
mental health 70, 74
morals 36, 37, 41, 46, 48, 53, 75, 77, 123, 166
mosaic approach 178

National Disability Reference Group 99
Neighbourhood Renewal Strategy 112
Netherlands 123
New Deal for Communities 112
New Zealand 87, 123
non-discrimination 46–7
Norway 14, 15, 105, 133, 147
nursery 78

Outer Mongolia 39, 56

parenting orders 24
Pakistan 37
periodic review of the UK Government (UNCRC) 36
play 5, 7, 13, 20, 25, 44, 67, 93, 100, 101, 112, 126, 140, 164, 171
policy 5, 9, 11, 13, 33, 49, 66, 70, 77, 86, 90, 105, 112
poverty 6, 11, 17, 20, 33, 54, 64, 77, 88, 95, 139, 140, 141, 144, 153, 161, 166
power 12, 21, 22, 26, 30, 38, 88, 92, 105, 126, 143, 145, 157, 179, 181
privacy 36, 43, 54, 62, 78, 81, 120, 152, 159
protection 138, 142, 145, 156
provision 62, 75, 77, 87, 140, 142, 163

Quality Protects 66, 99, 109, 112

race 5, 20, 31, 41, 88, 95, 98, 176
Ready Steady Change 20
religion 7, 34, 37, 38, 45, 47, 62, 87, 137–8, 147, 148–50, 161
research 6, 7–12, 14–16, 34–5, 39, 51, 62–3, 64–6, 73–6, 78–81, 92–7, 99–108, 113, 119–30, 151–6, 160–1, 171–8

rights
  as concept 19, 27, 30, 34, 65
  and the EU 7, 9, 11
  and human rights 40–2
  and liberty 30–3, 34, 39, 40, 41, 42, 46,
    49, 50, 53, 55, 152, 157, 158
  and participation 70, 90, 117, 119, 133,
    138, 145, 155–7
  and protection 138, 142, 145, 156
  and provision 62, 75, 77, 87, 140, 142,
    163
  and the rights agenda 13, 16, 17, 20, 27,
    49, 72, 79, 108, 189
  and the rights dynamic 13, 14, 16, 19,
    26, 28, 49, 80
  and the UNCRC 5, 6, 7, 12, 14, 15, 23,
    25, 27, 42–8, 53, 54, 57, 65–70, 72, 77,
    90, 118, 136–7, 150–2, 155, 167
  and welfare 24, 25–37, 39, 40, 41–2, 46,
    50, 53, 55, 70, 75, 110, 117, 134, 137,
    153, 157

Save the Children 6, 10, 40, 57, 144, 160, 183
Scotland 98, 142, 157, 185
sex 7, 24, 47, 137, 148, 171
sexuality 5, 20, 73, 88, 140, 170, 180
shelter 36, 140, 174
smacking *see* violence
Social Care Institute for Excellence
  (SCIE) 130, 133
social inclusion 18, 64, 132
social services 151, 155, 170
social status 7
somaj 34

space 13, 25, 91, 115, 117, 121, 131, 146,
  169, 171, 173
status 34, 47, 52, 62, 72, 88, 89–90, 98, 114,
  139, 152, 157, 171, 176
Sudan 164
Sweden 17, 54, 157

time 126, 146, 153, 161, 172

Unicef 37, 135
United Nations Committee on the Rights
  of the Child 79, 186
United Nations Convention on the Rights
  of the Child 5, 6, 7, 12, 14, 15, 23, 25,
  27, 53, 54, 57, 65–70, 72, 77, 90, 118,
  136–7, 152, 155, 167
United States of America 34, 46, 152
Universal Declaration of Human
  Rights 41, 42, 49, 77, 110

violence 7, 11, 43, 70, 77, 161
  and smacking 9, 12, 25, 152
voice 11, 21, 23, 51, 85
vulnerability 49, 52, 64

war 6, 23, 41, 44, 164, 166
welfare 24, 25–37, 39, 40–2, 46, 50, 53, 55,
  70, 75, 110, 114, 117, 134, 137, 153,
  157
Western Culture 150–1

youth 6, 21, 24, 86, 106, 109, 113–16,
  119–34, 161, 169, 185
Youth on Board 114, 116